This book belongs to the collection of

Published by

"GDG©"

Global Doodle Gems

Share your colored versions with us ! We love seeing your results and hearing from you we are social !

The Official FB book page, stay on top of what we have in the works !
www.facebook.com/globaldoodlegems
The Community group, share your colored pages, meet the artists, enjoy exclusive freebies, take part in community Charity books and so much more......
www.facebook.com/groups/globaldoodlegems/
Follow us on Twitter.... @GlobalDoodlegem
We are on Instagram too
@globaldoodlegems for instagram
...and if you are not social like that we have a blog
globaldoodlegems.wordpress.com

All of us from the Global Doodle Gems wish you a colortastic time and look forward to seeing your wonderful color results online !

Love The Patterns

These Heart Designs I made with Love and Valentines in Mind ...
hopefully you will find them great for expressing your love...
or even dreaming of love !
The series of Designs consist of 3 types of Designs
1. Abstract Love
2. Lovely'Dala's
3. Love the patterns
There are 3 books with each specific type and a 4th called
Never Too Many Hearts with all 150 designs
for those that want the full set !
I hope you will enjoy coloring these drawings of mine
and that they will help you relax and find inner peace
and joy with your colors !

I wish to thank
Johanna Ans and Manuela Bremer
from the buttom of my heart for their
lovely colorings for the cover art work !
Maria Wedel

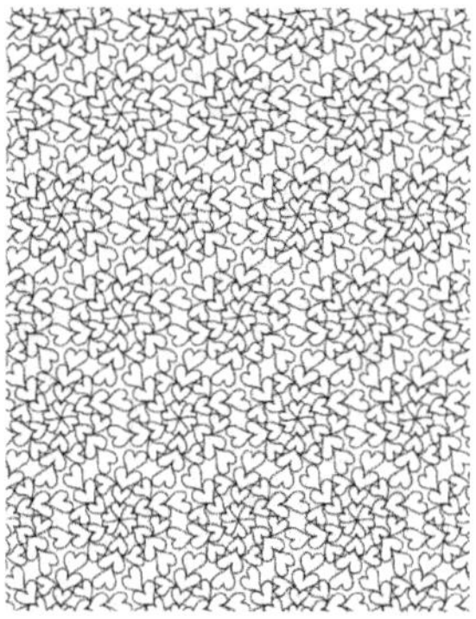
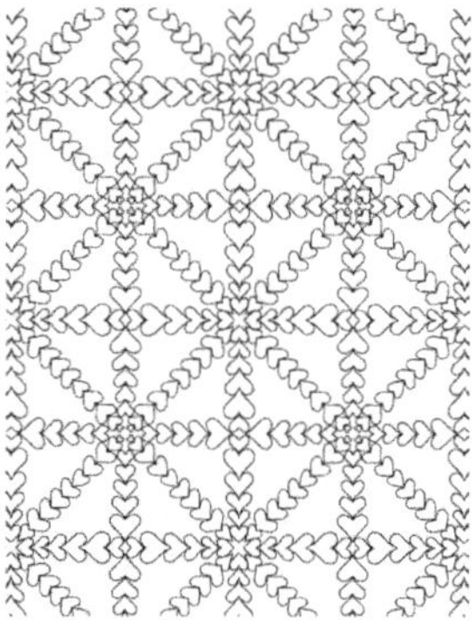
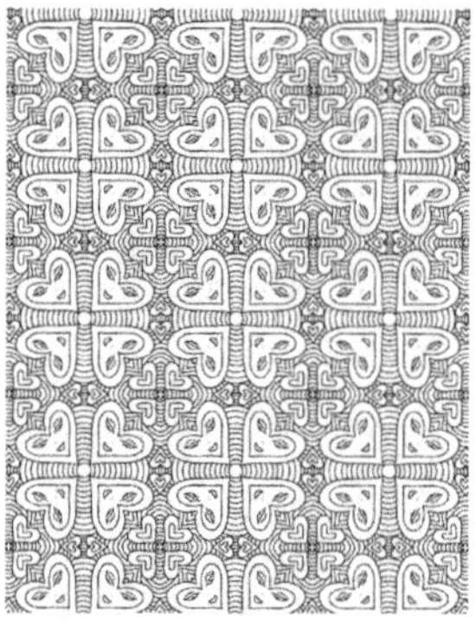
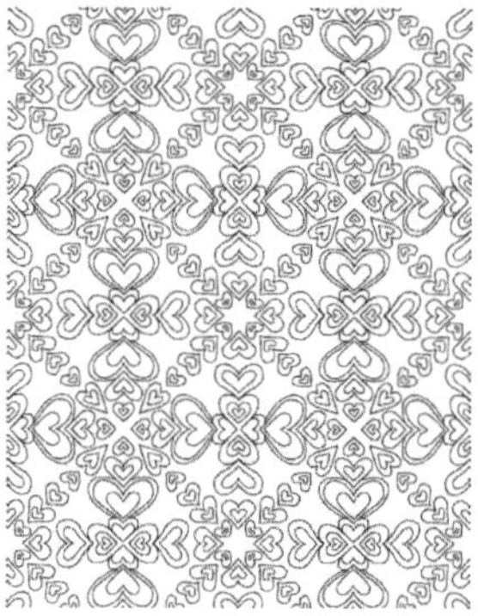
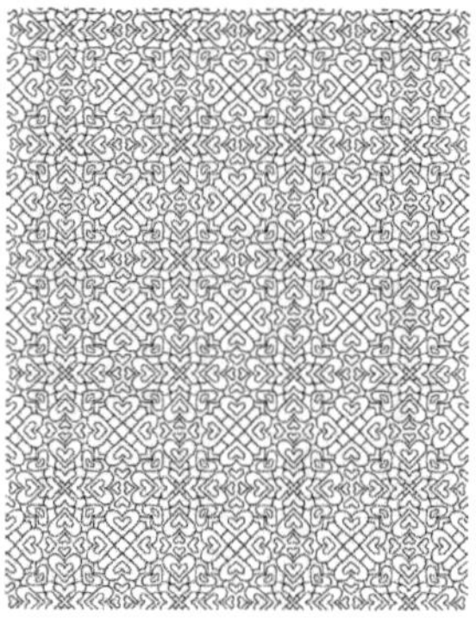
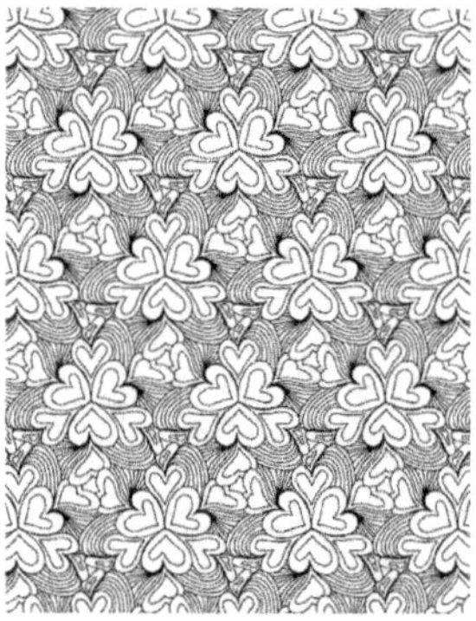
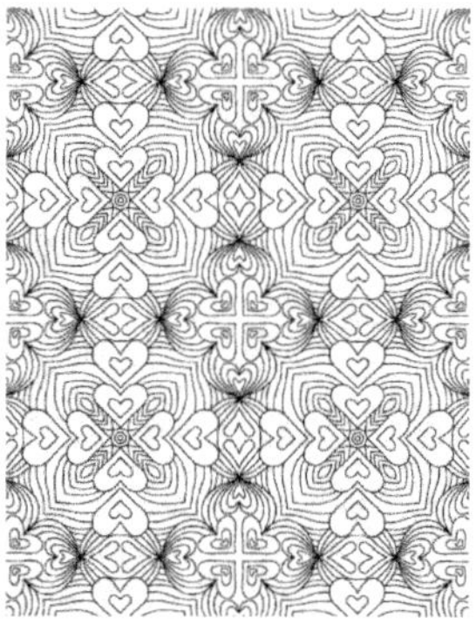
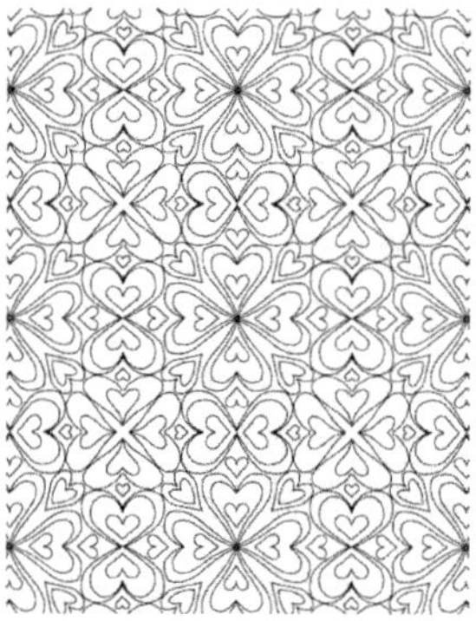
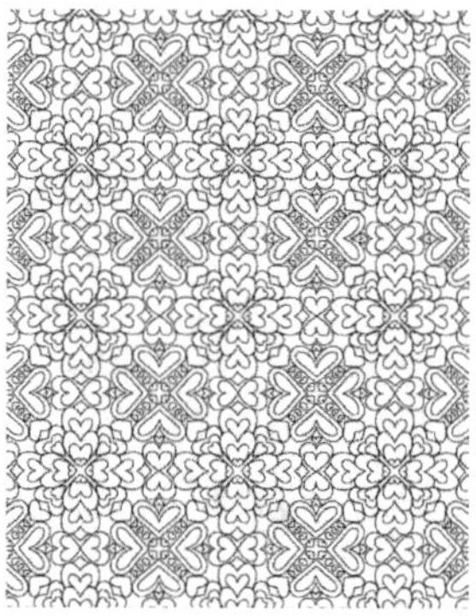
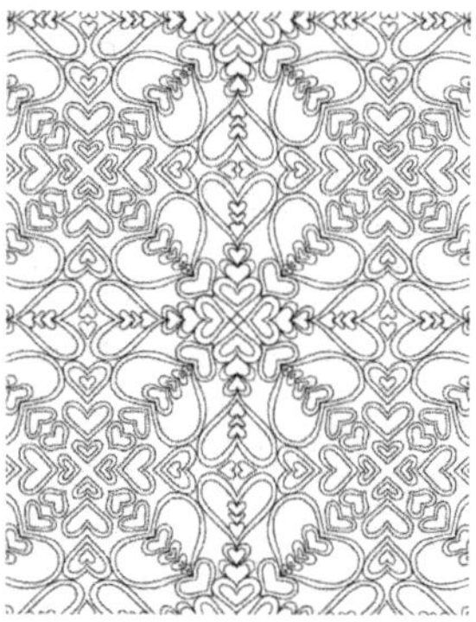
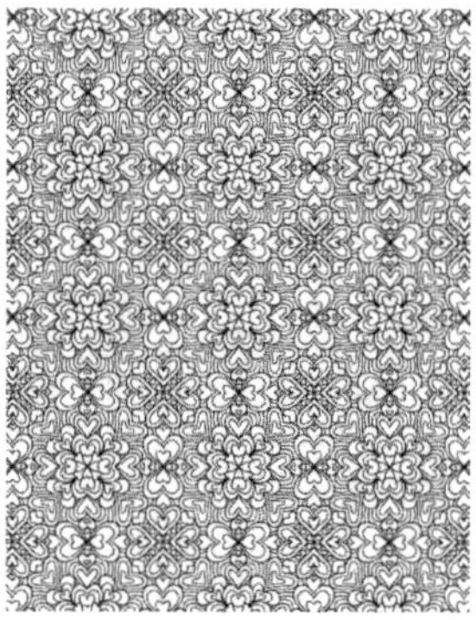
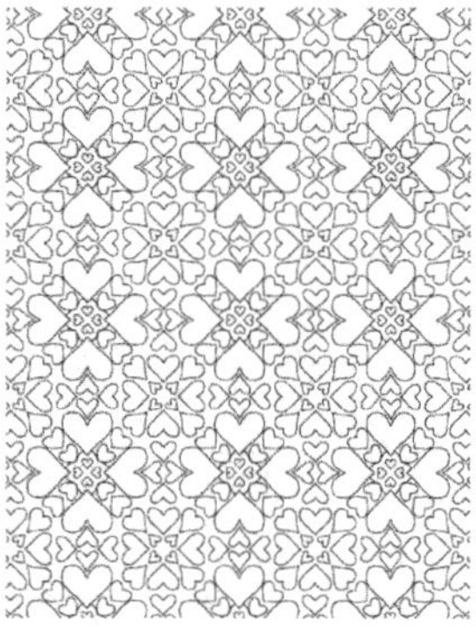
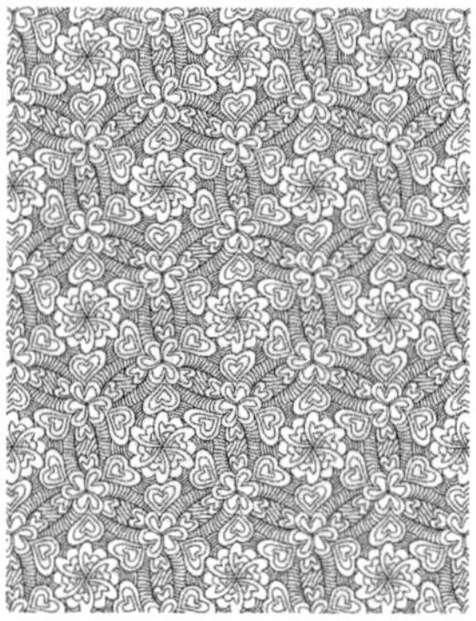
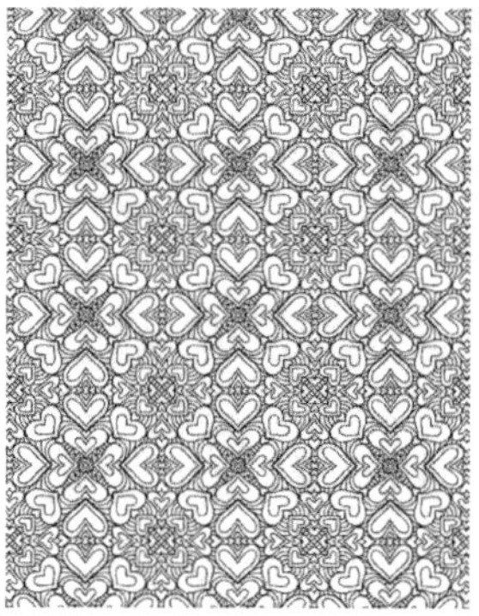
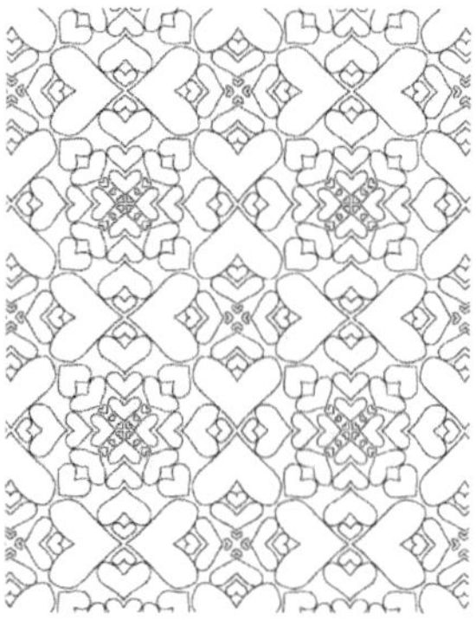
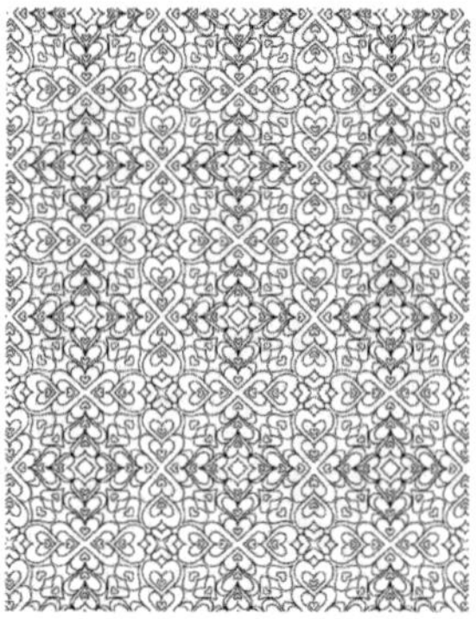
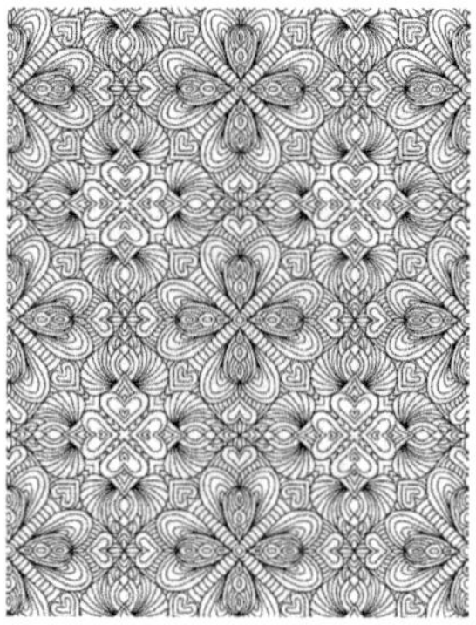
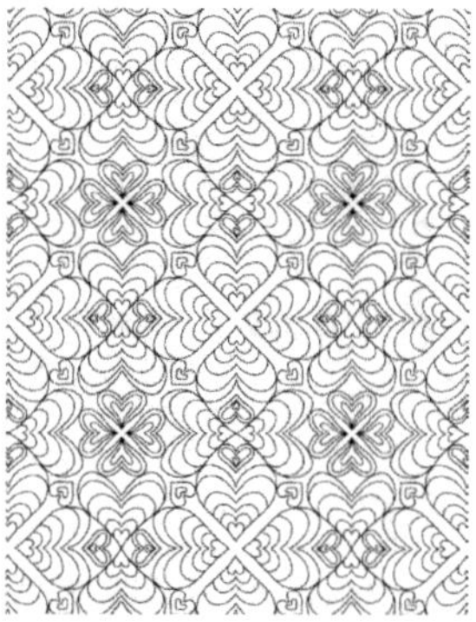
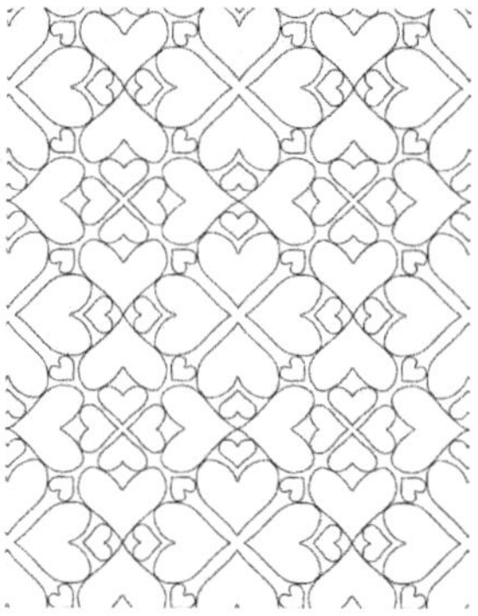
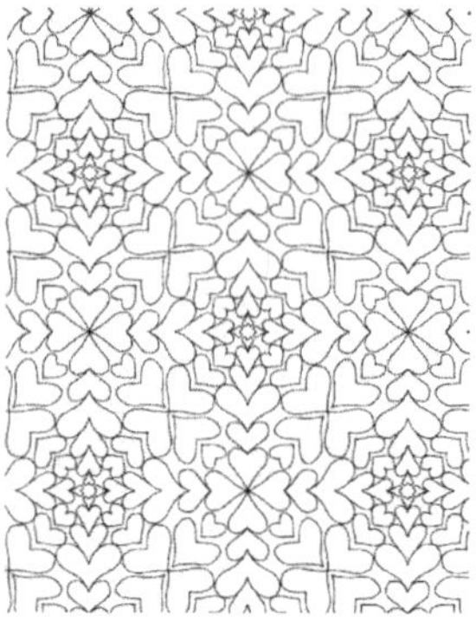
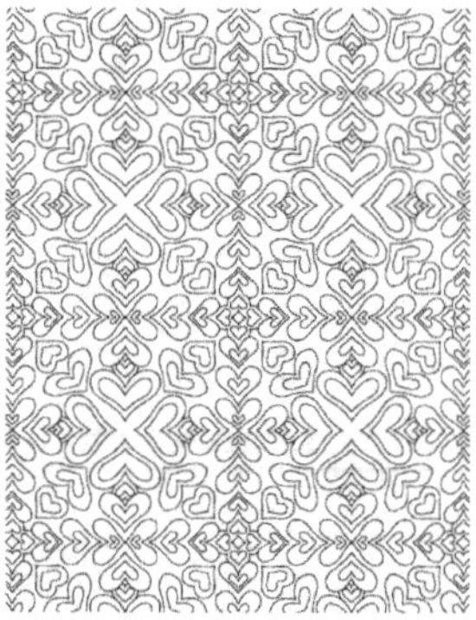
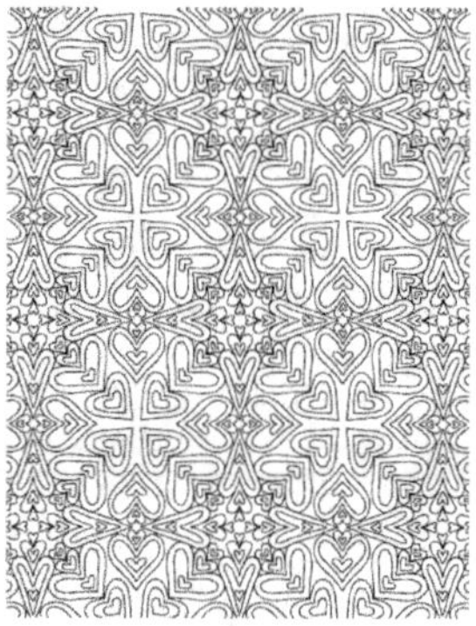
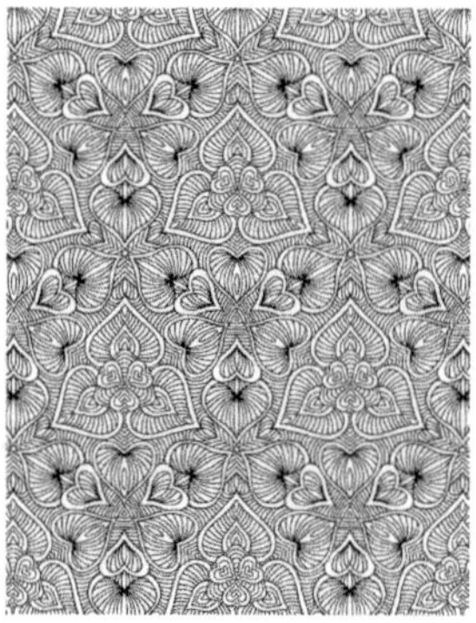
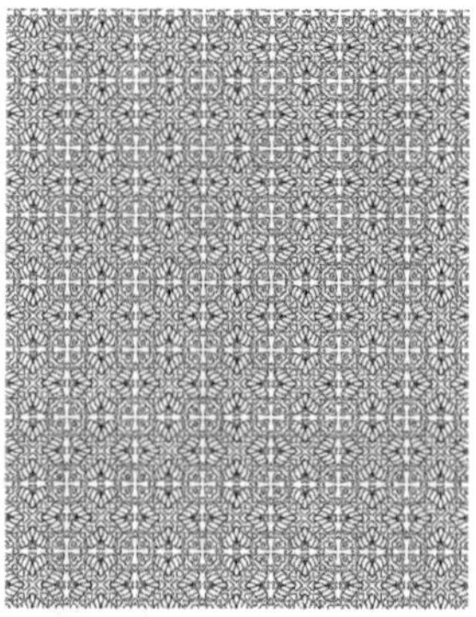
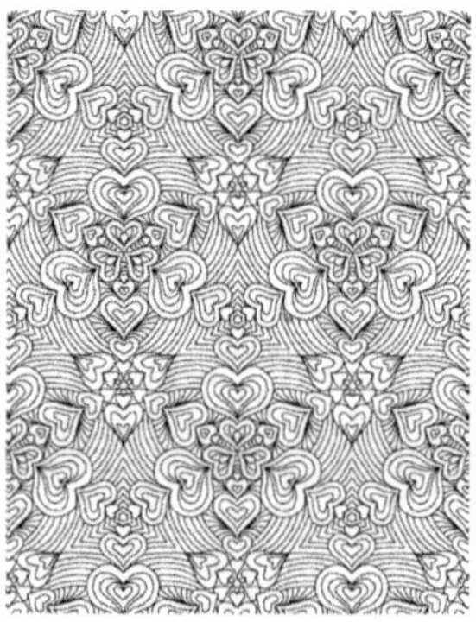

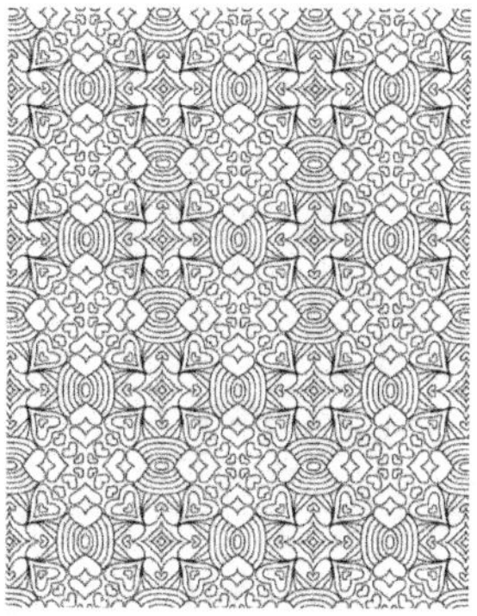
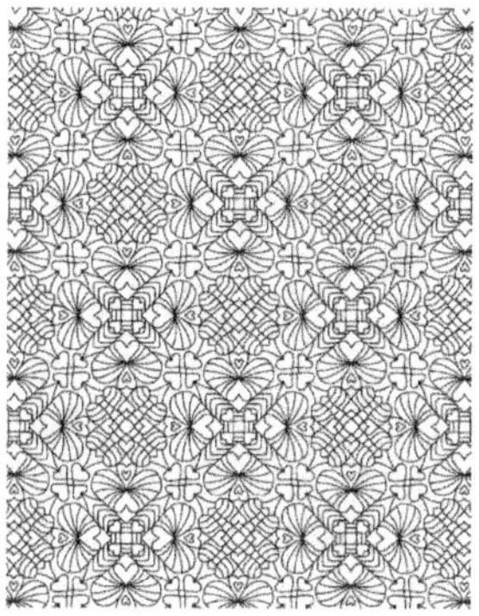
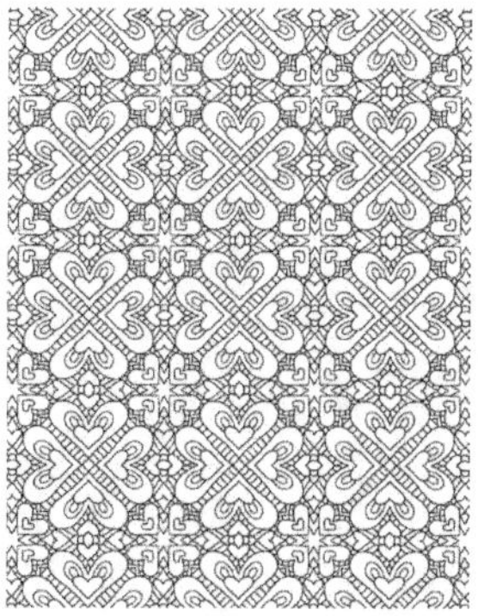
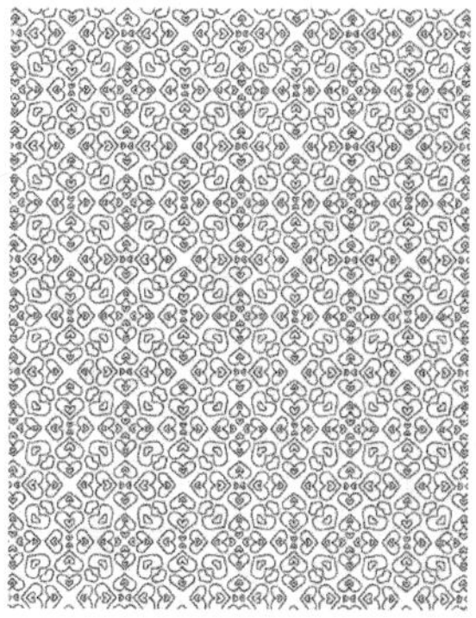
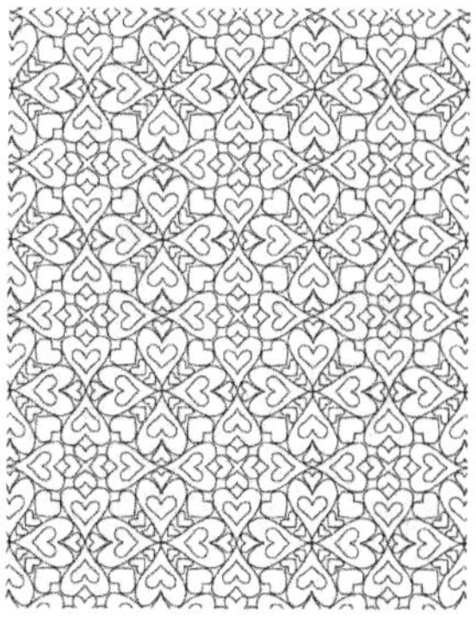
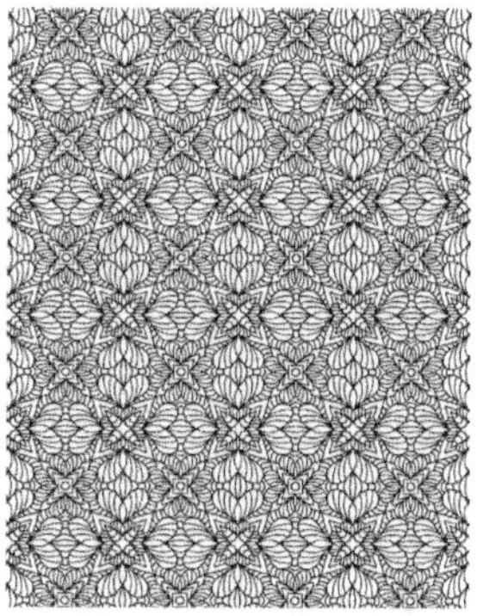
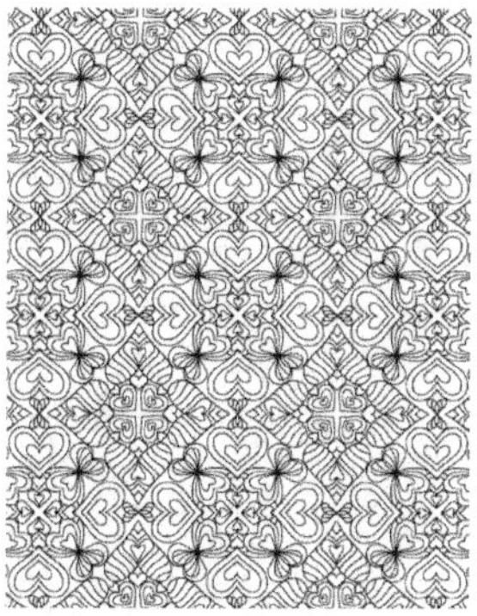
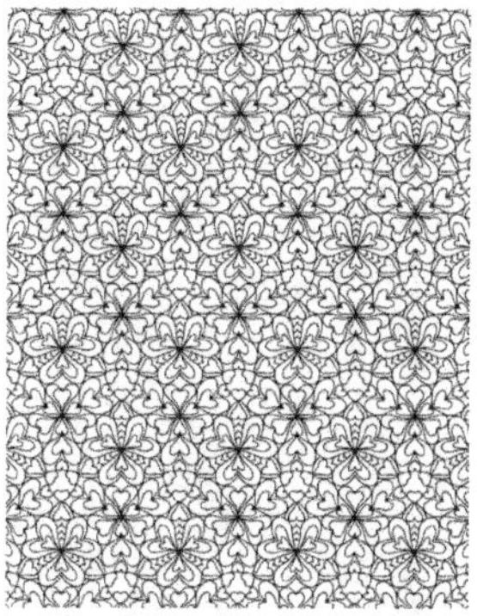
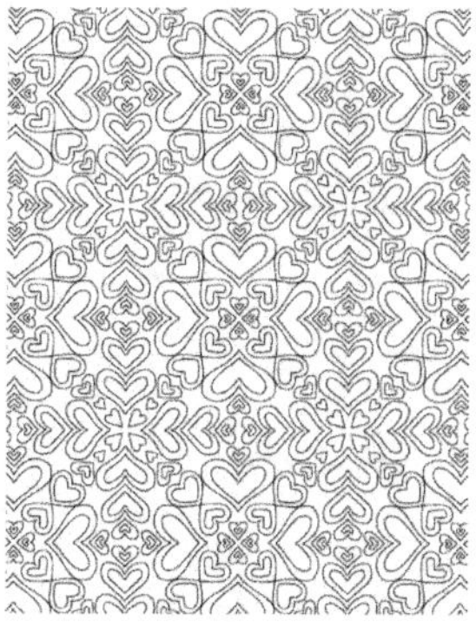
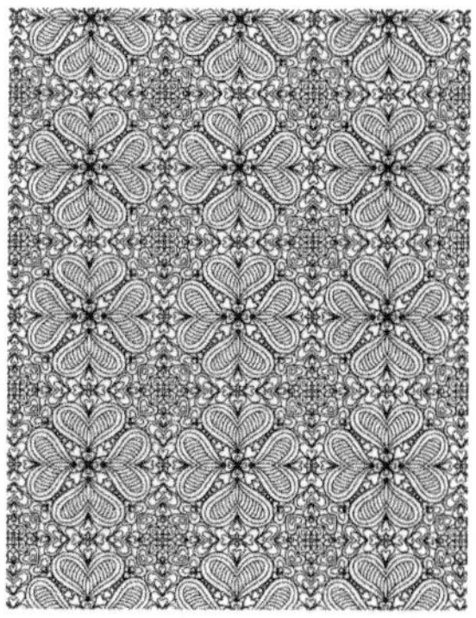
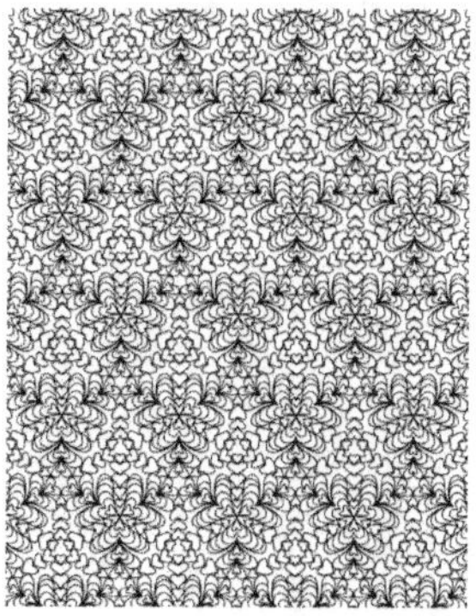
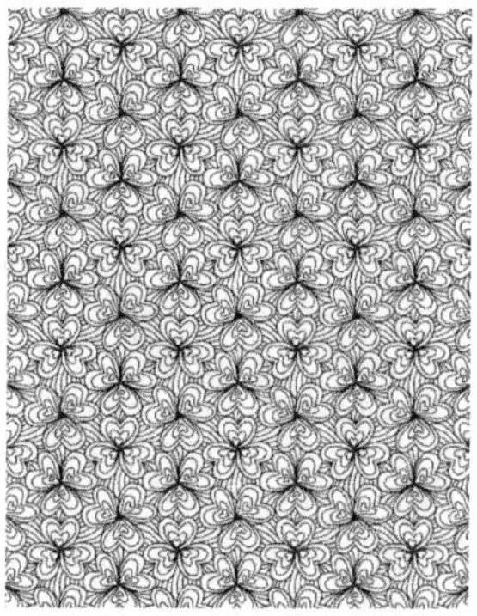
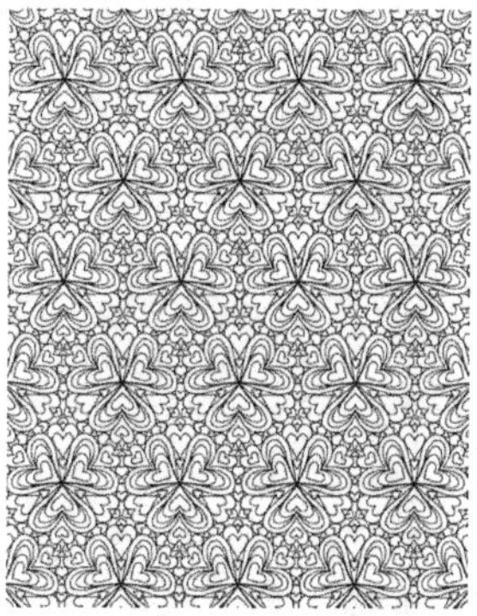
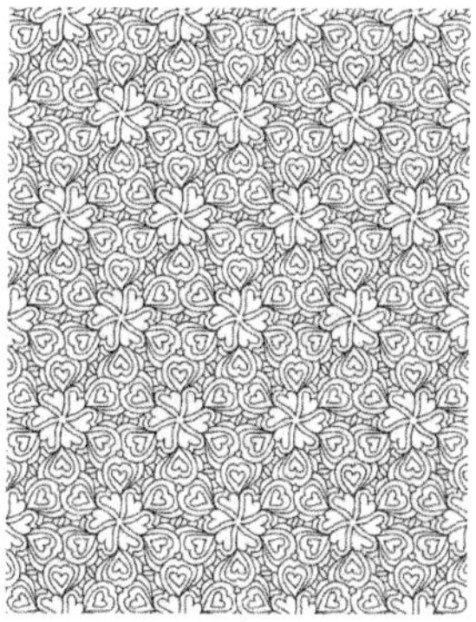
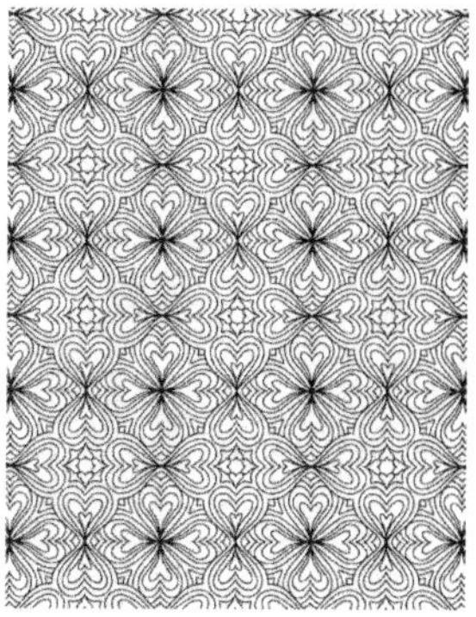
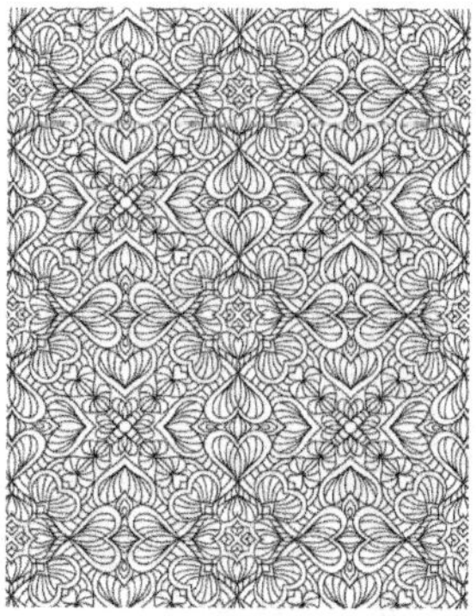
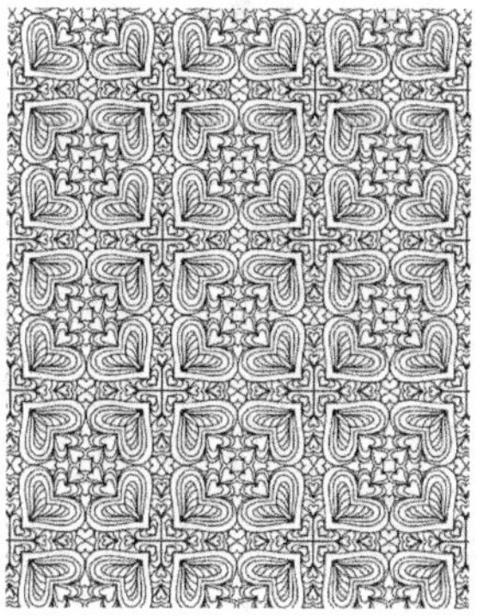
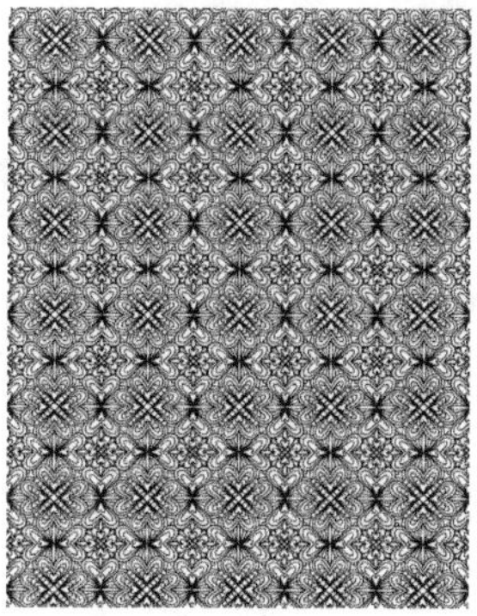
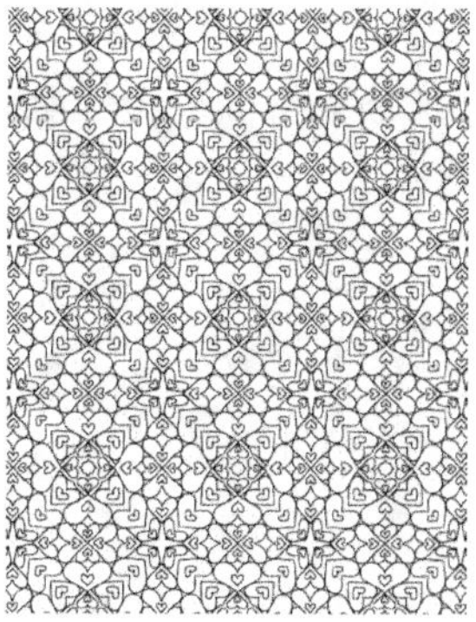
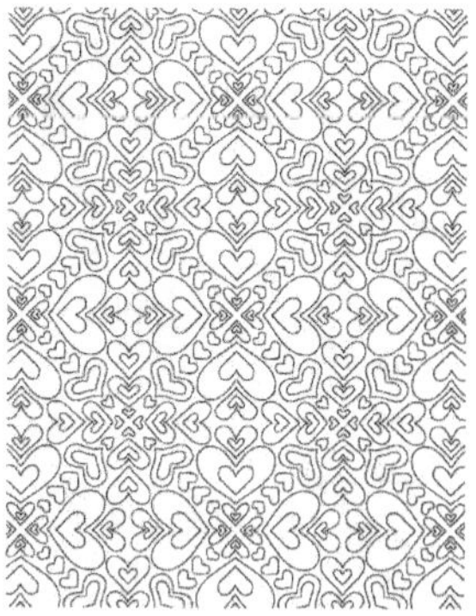
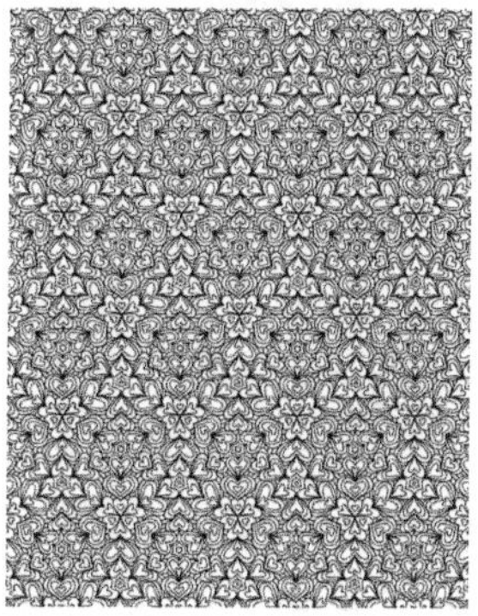
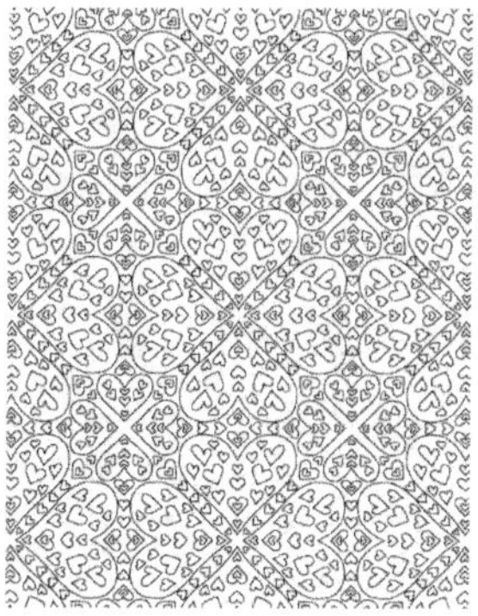
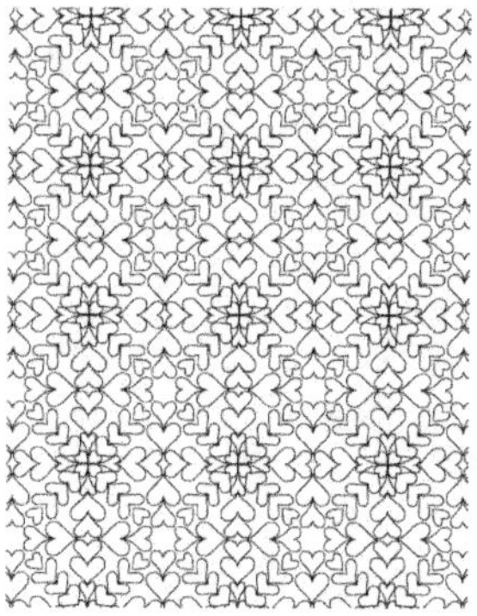
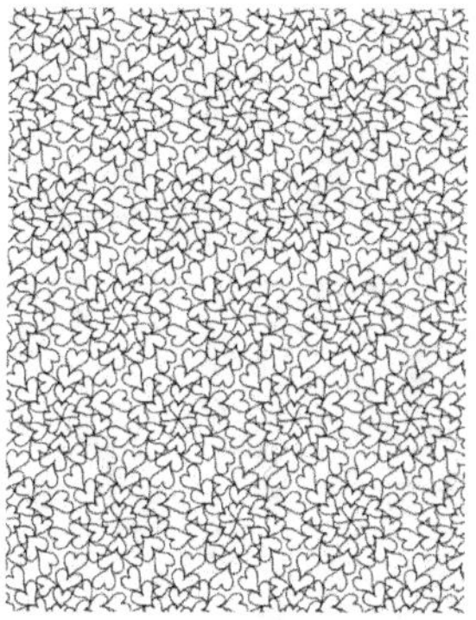
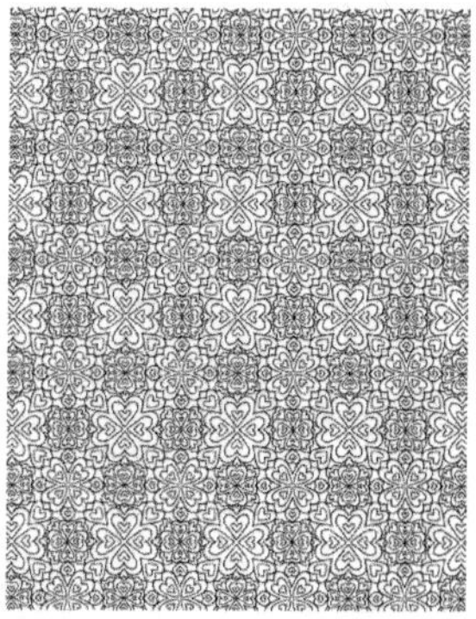

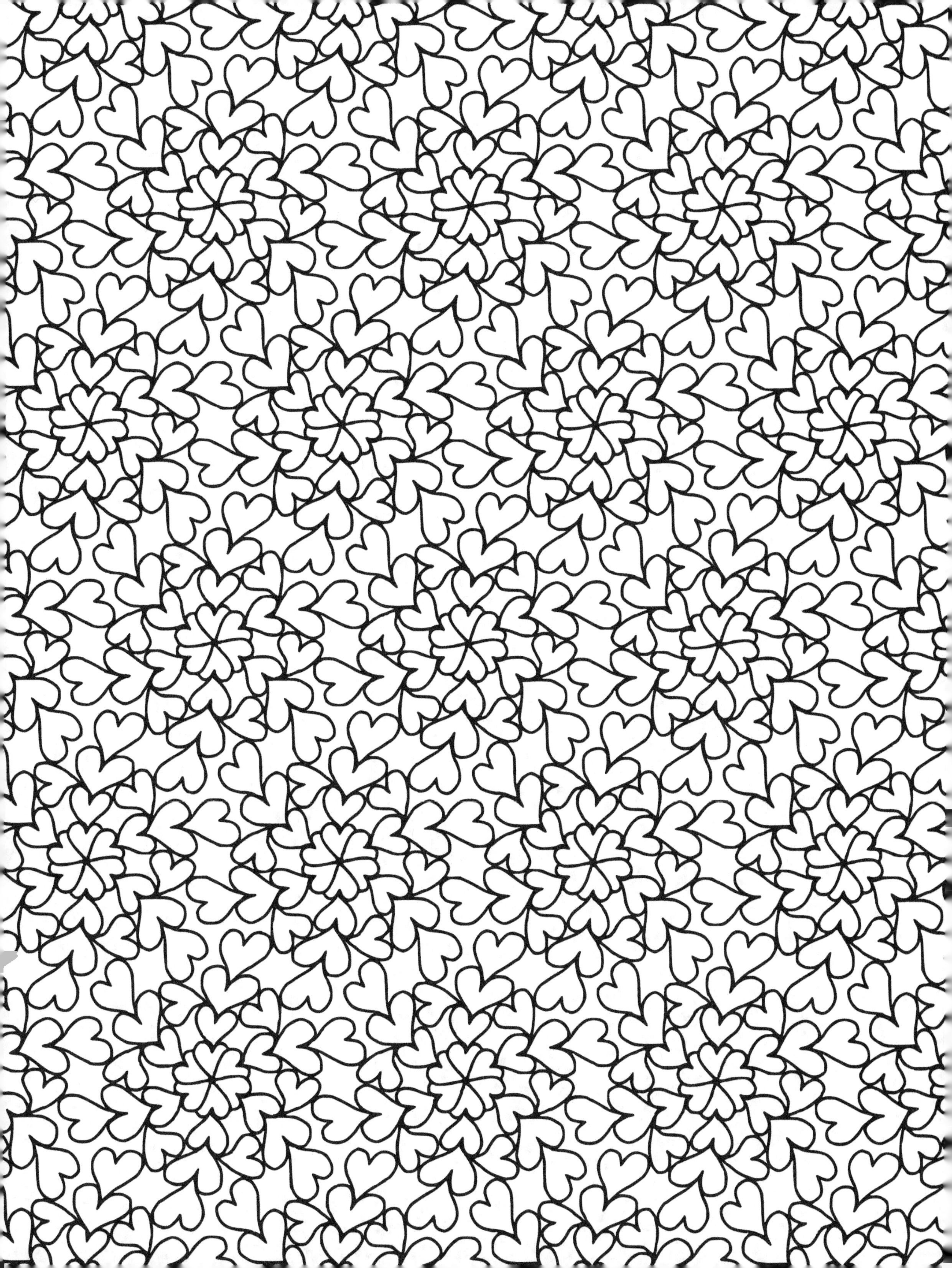

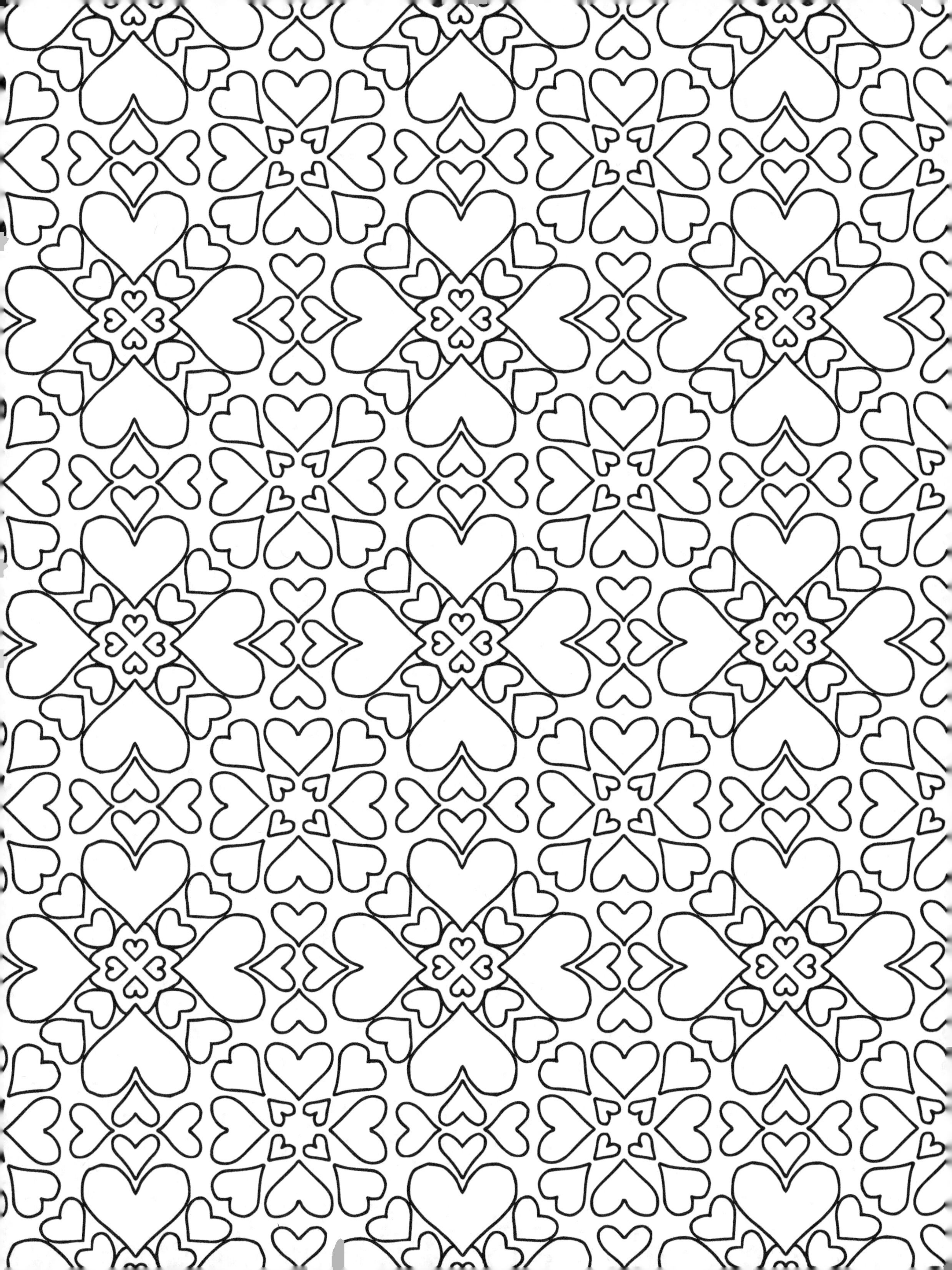

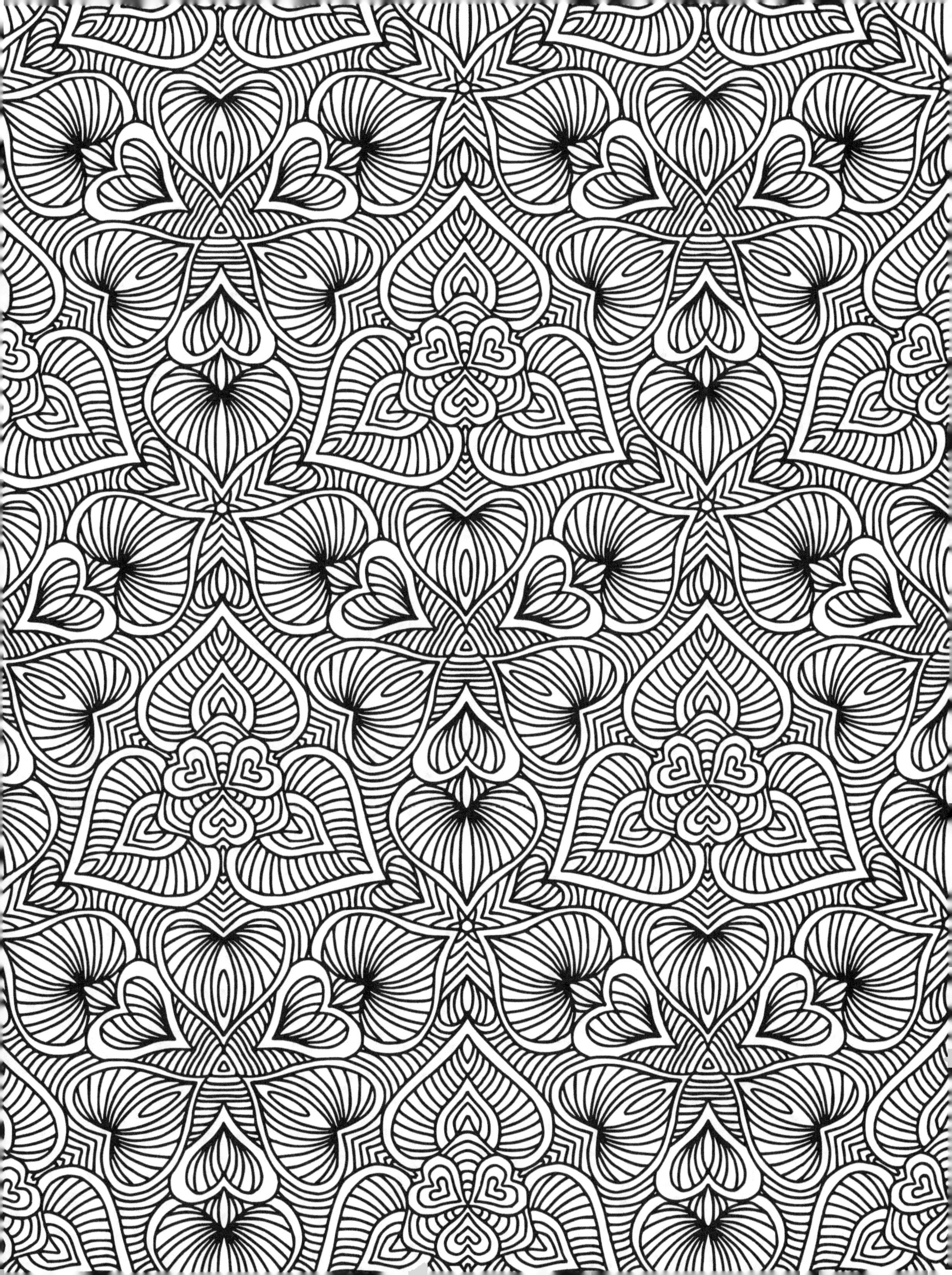

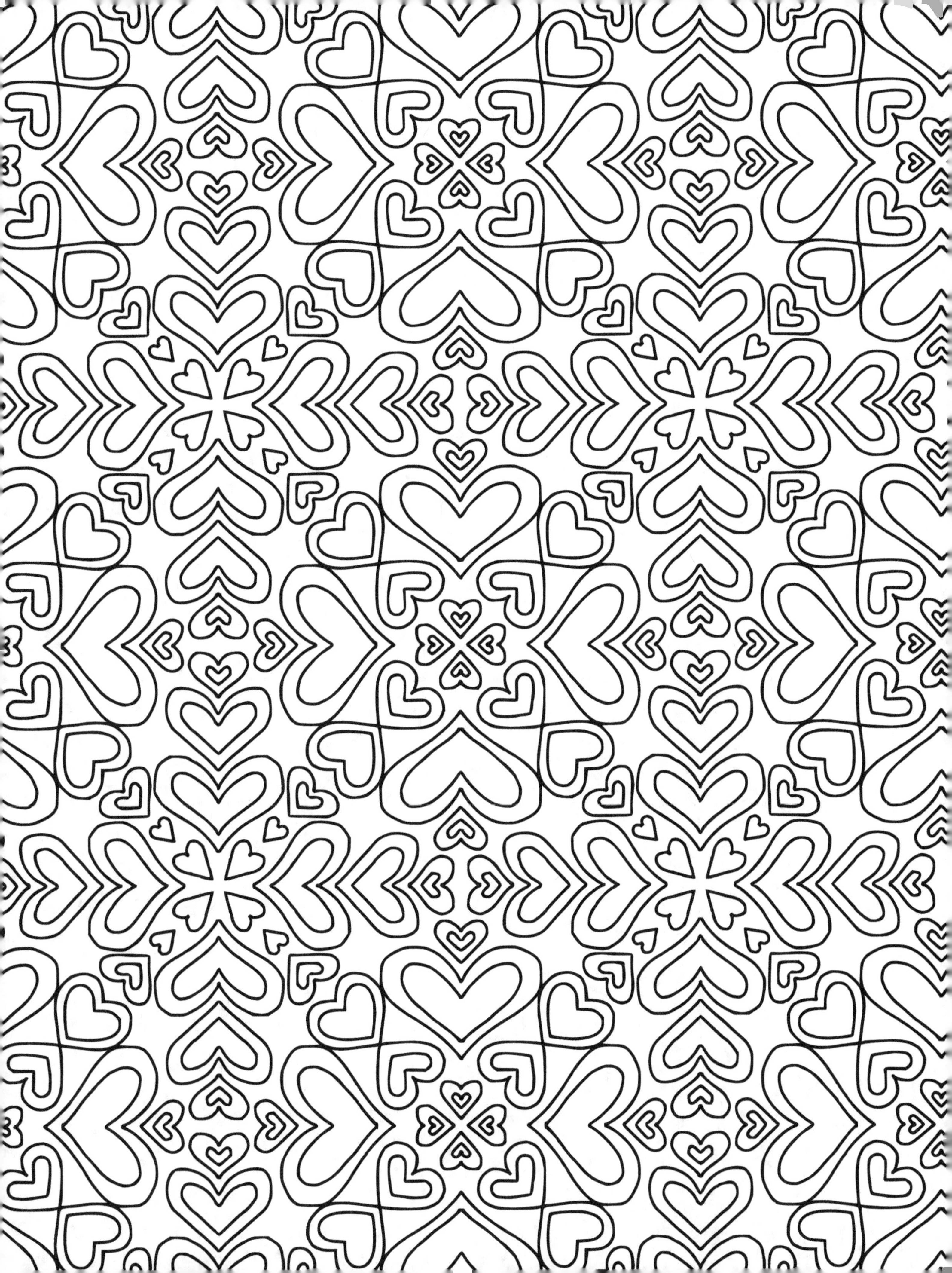

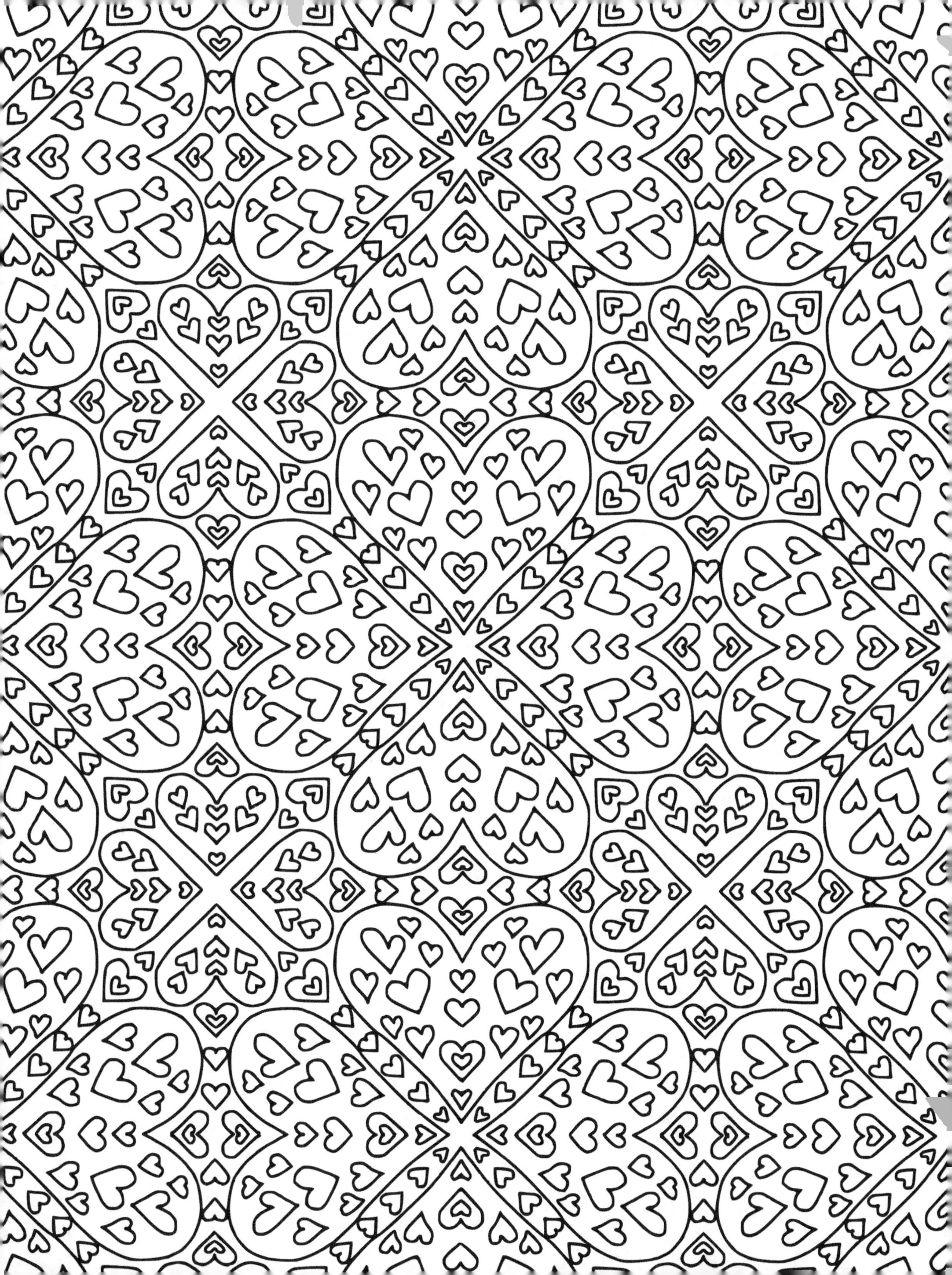

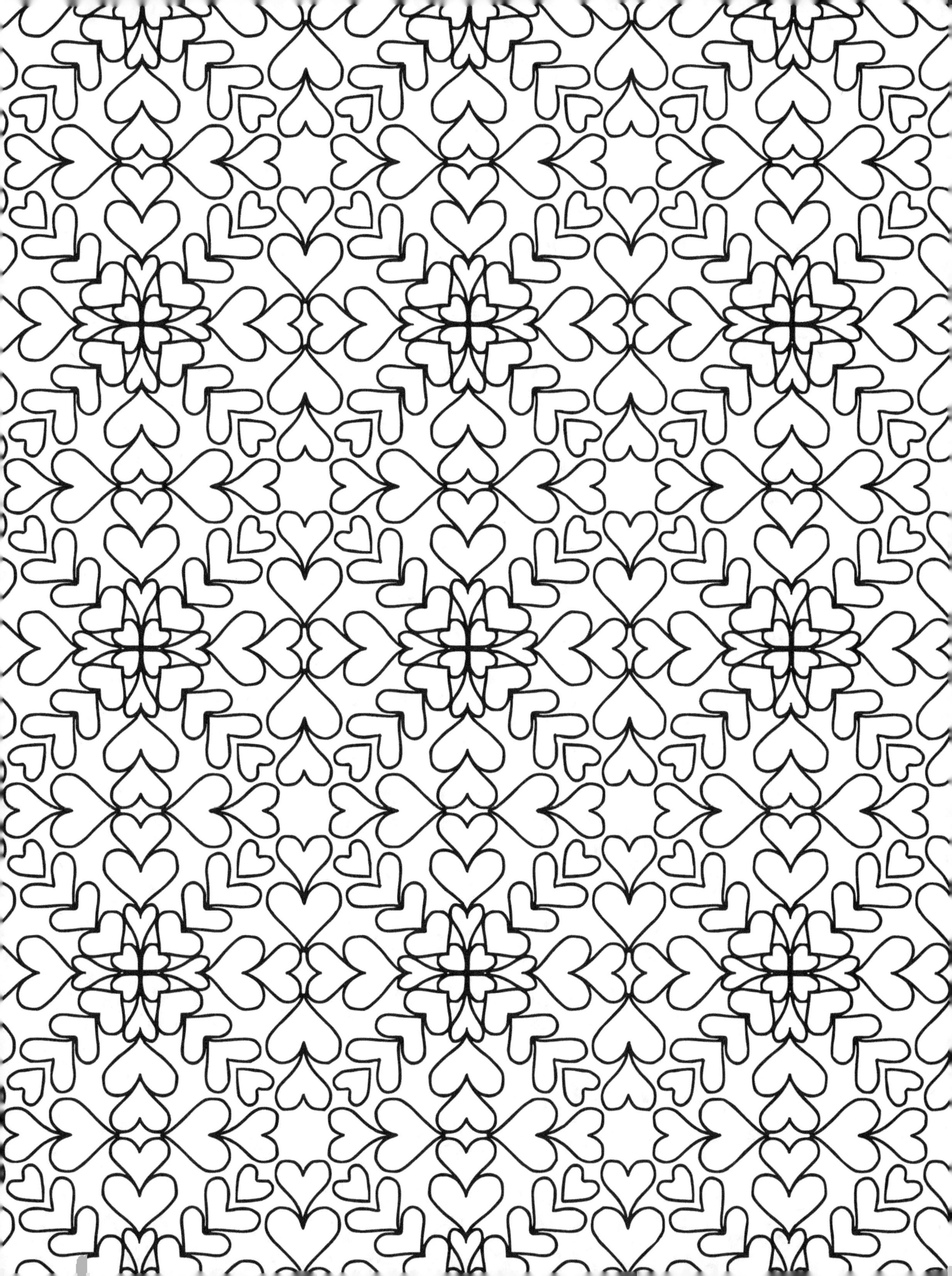

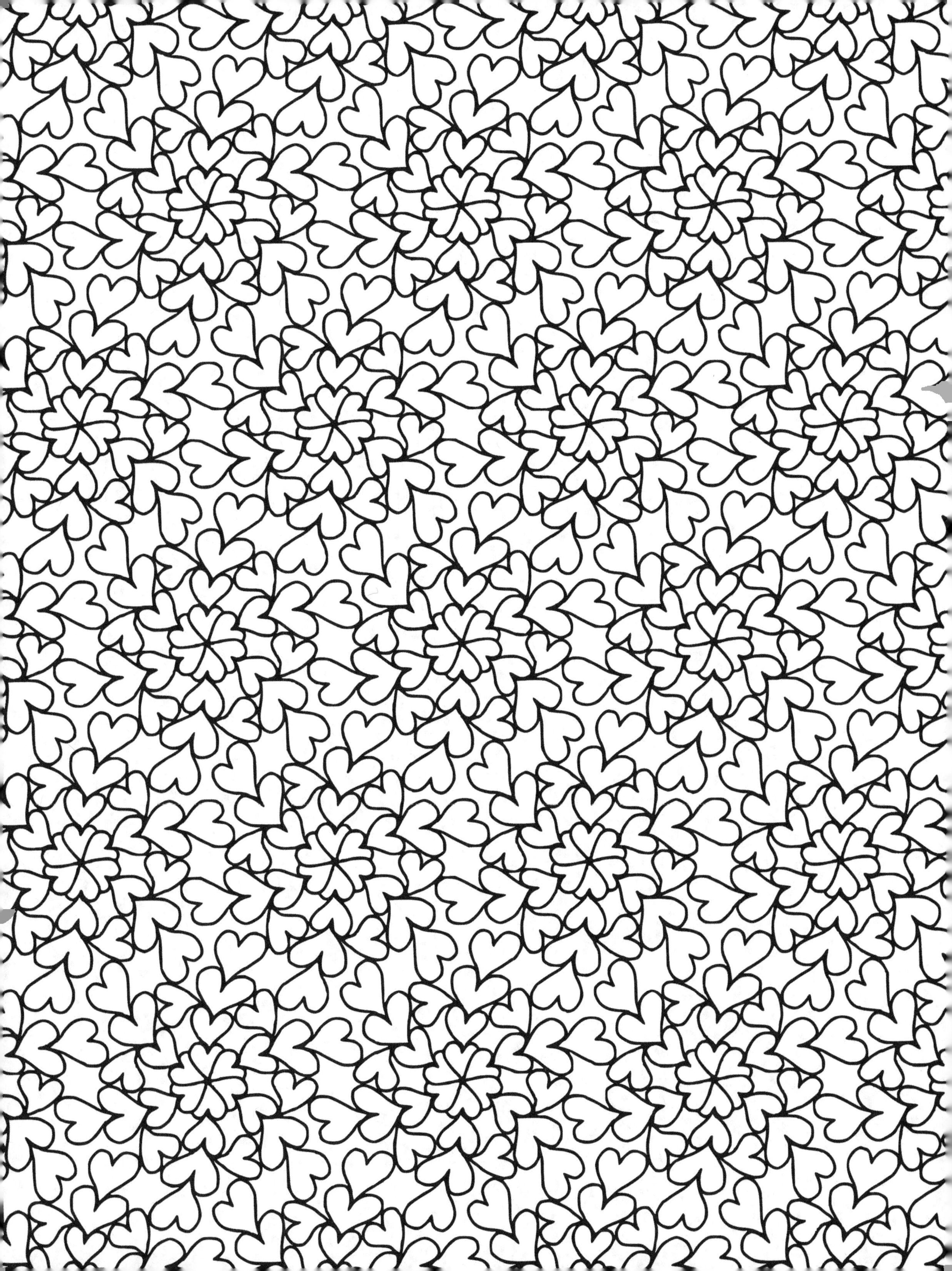

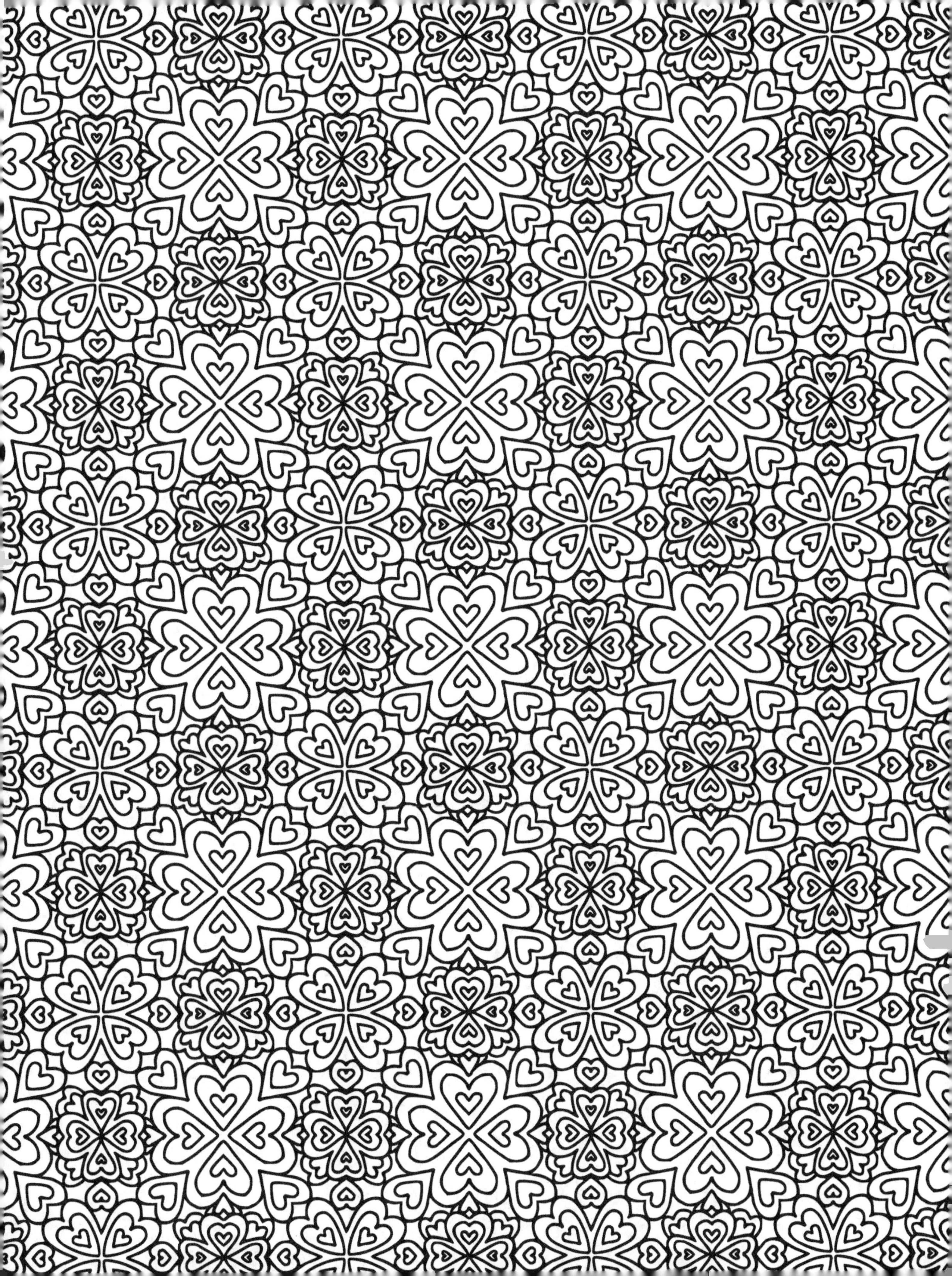

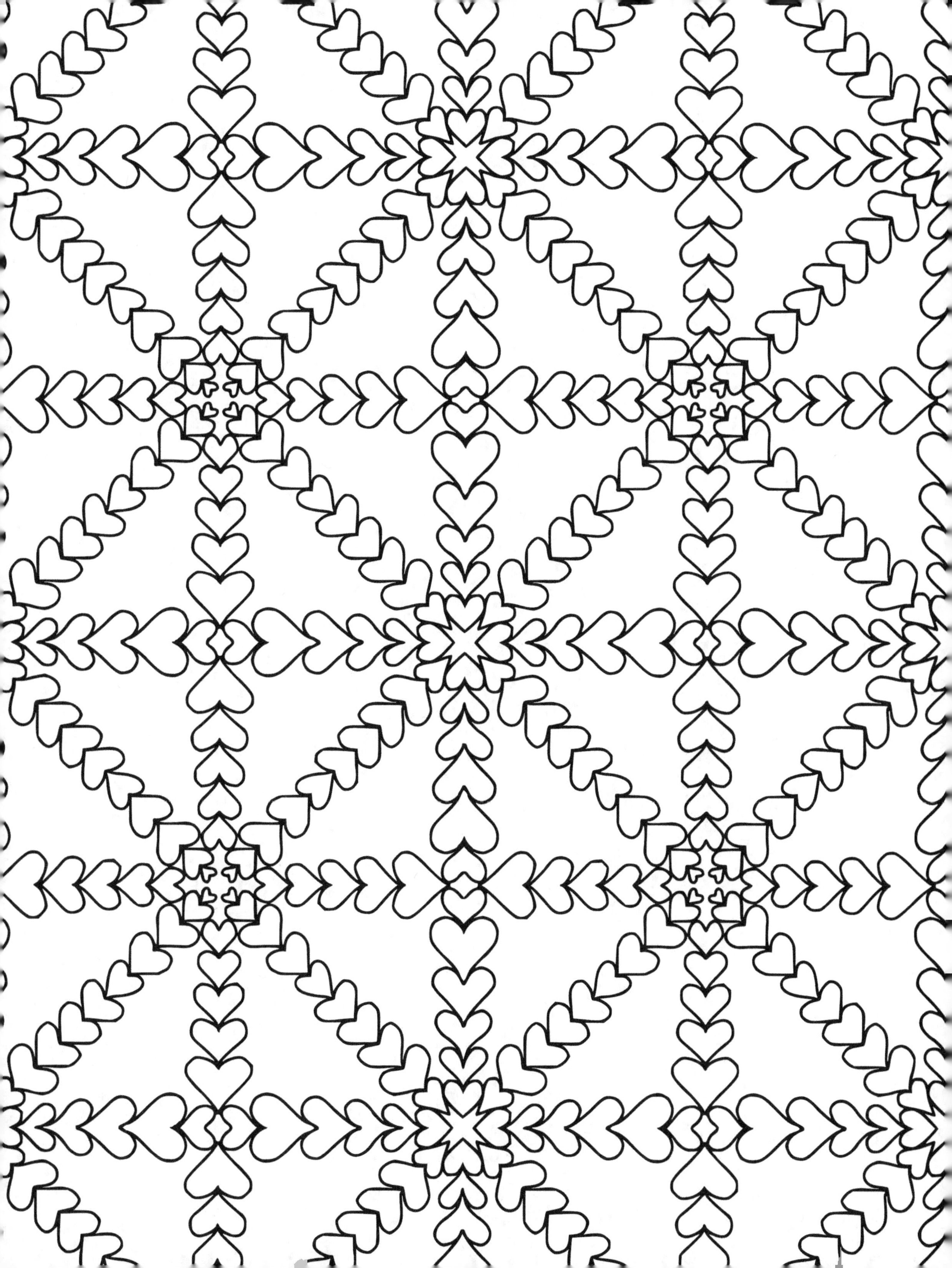

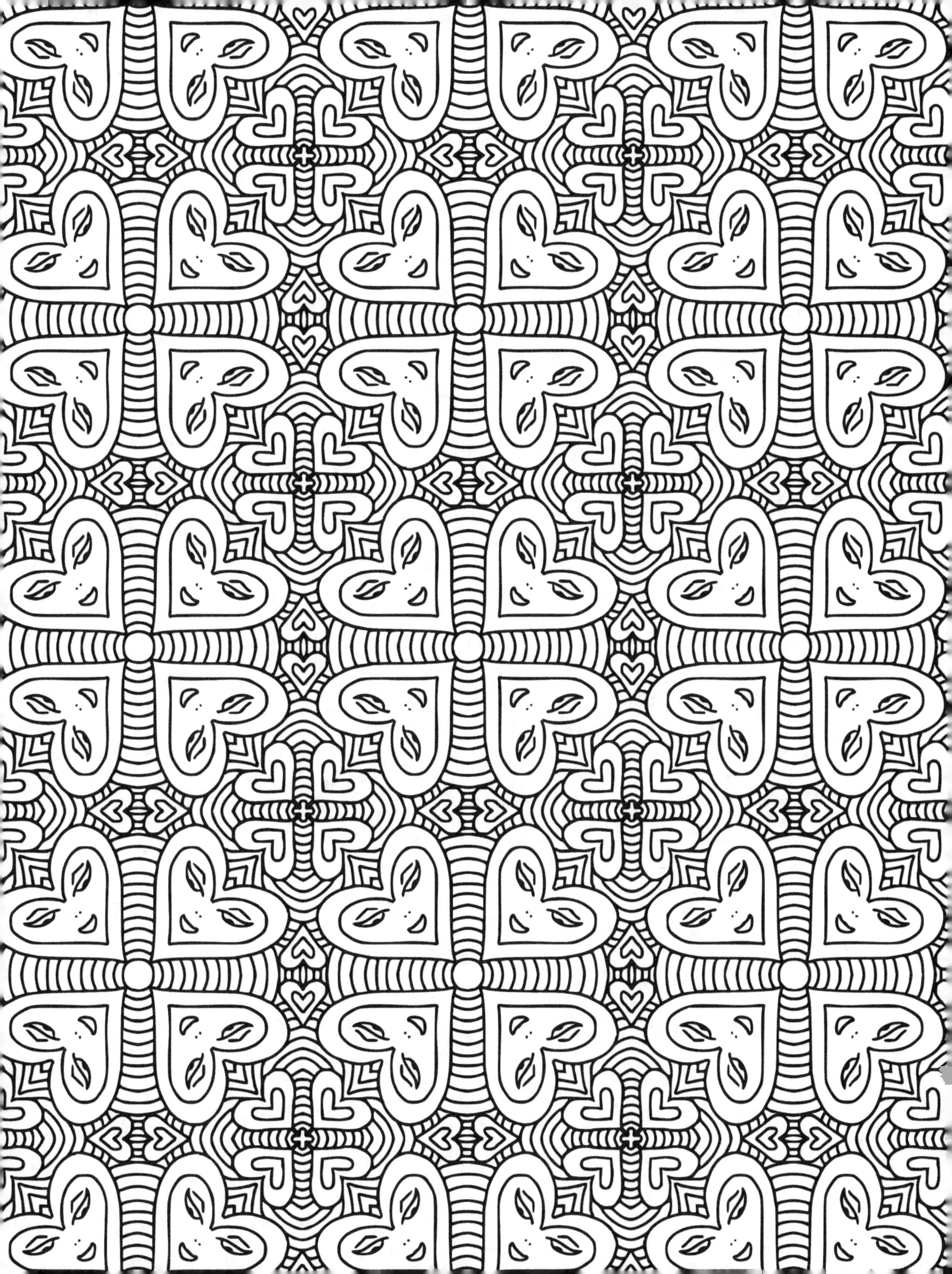

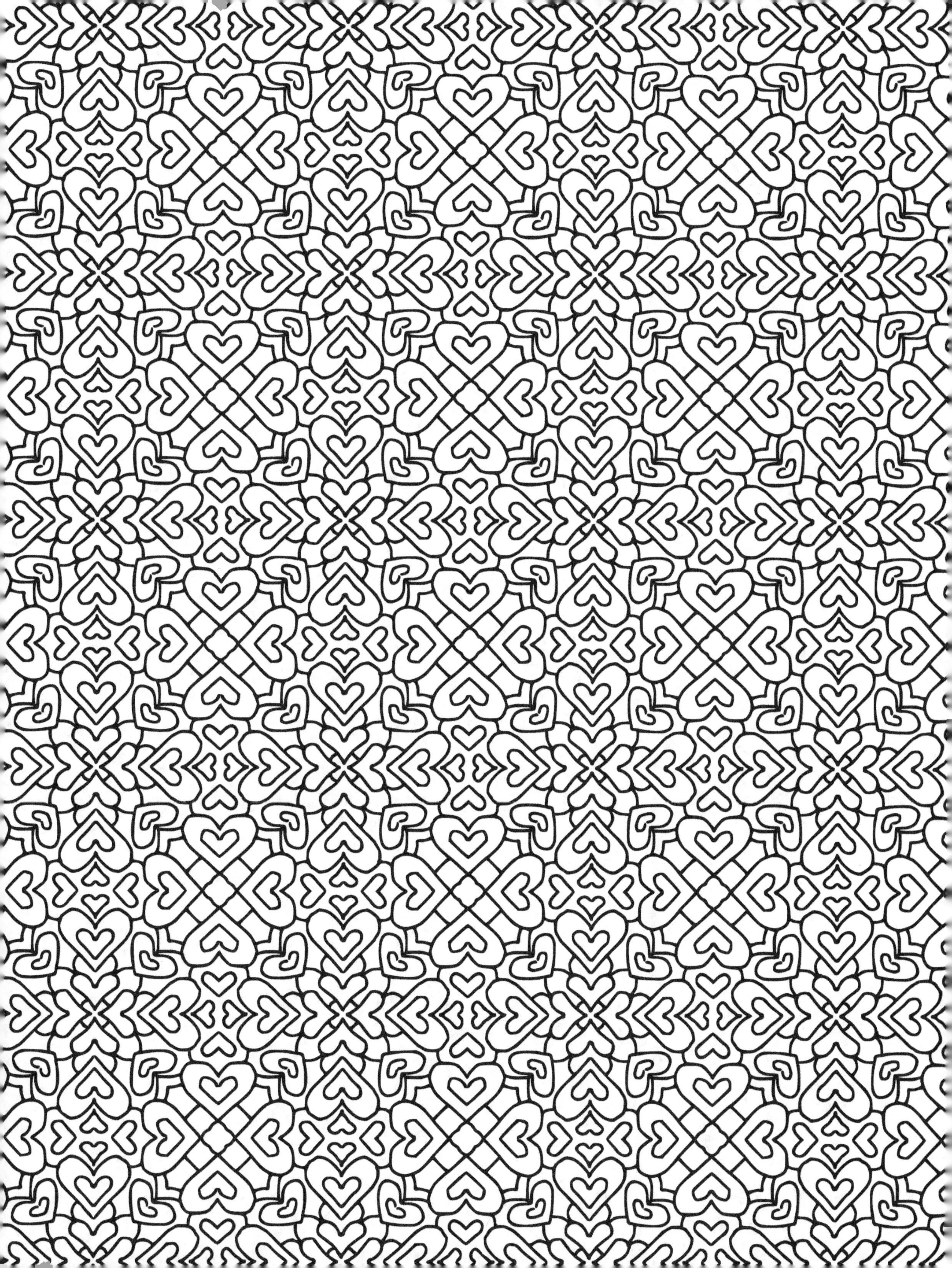

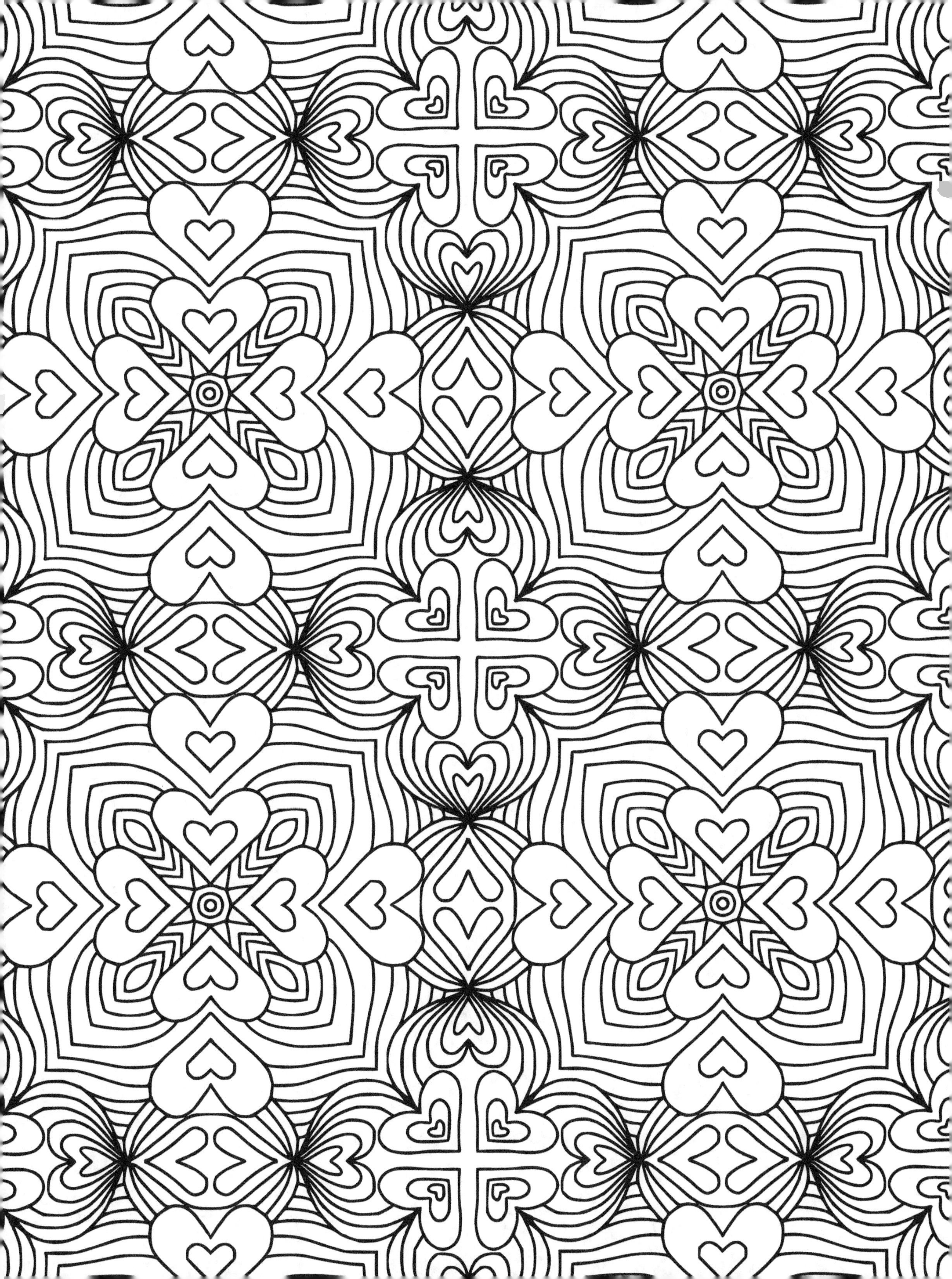

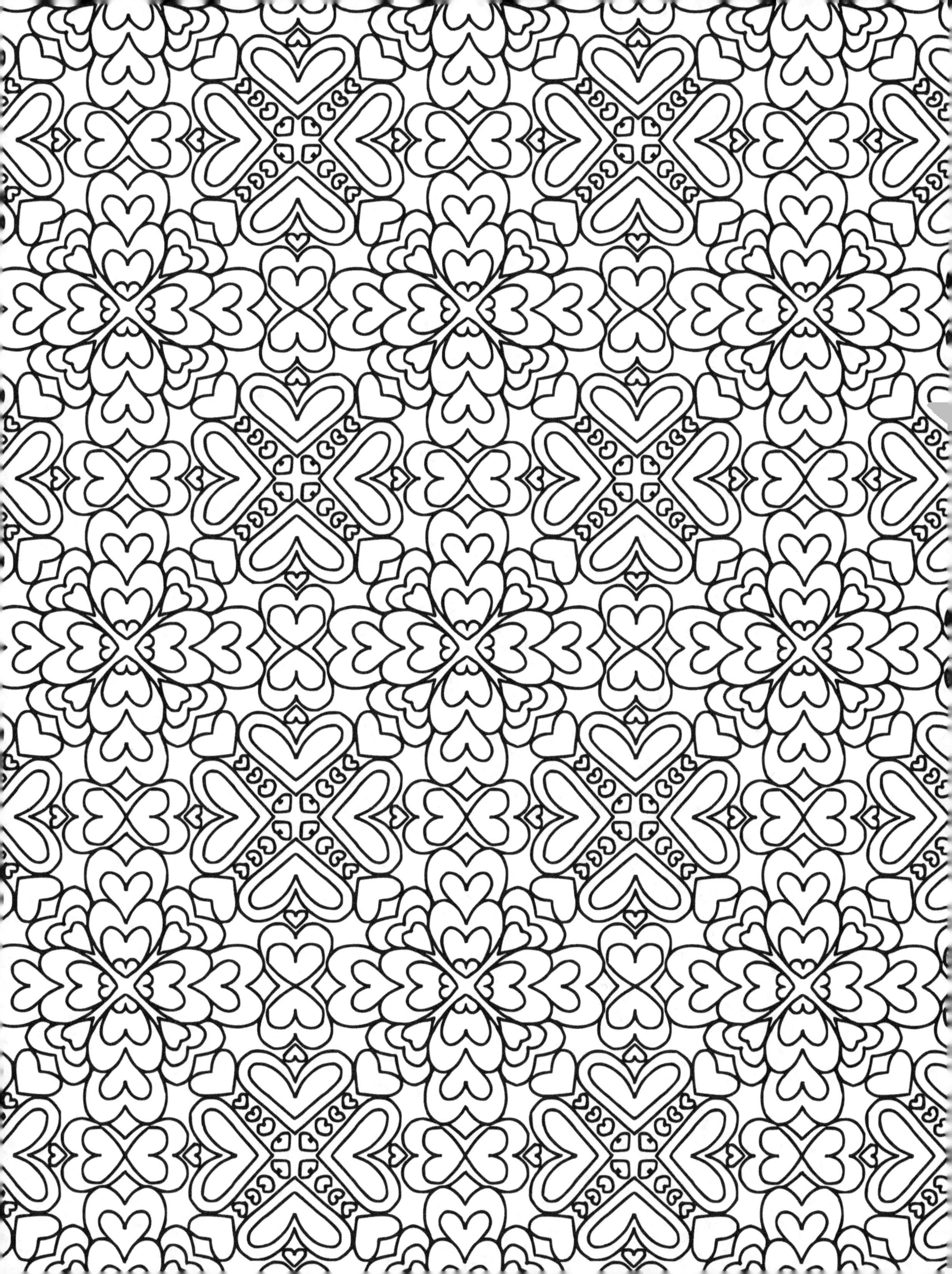

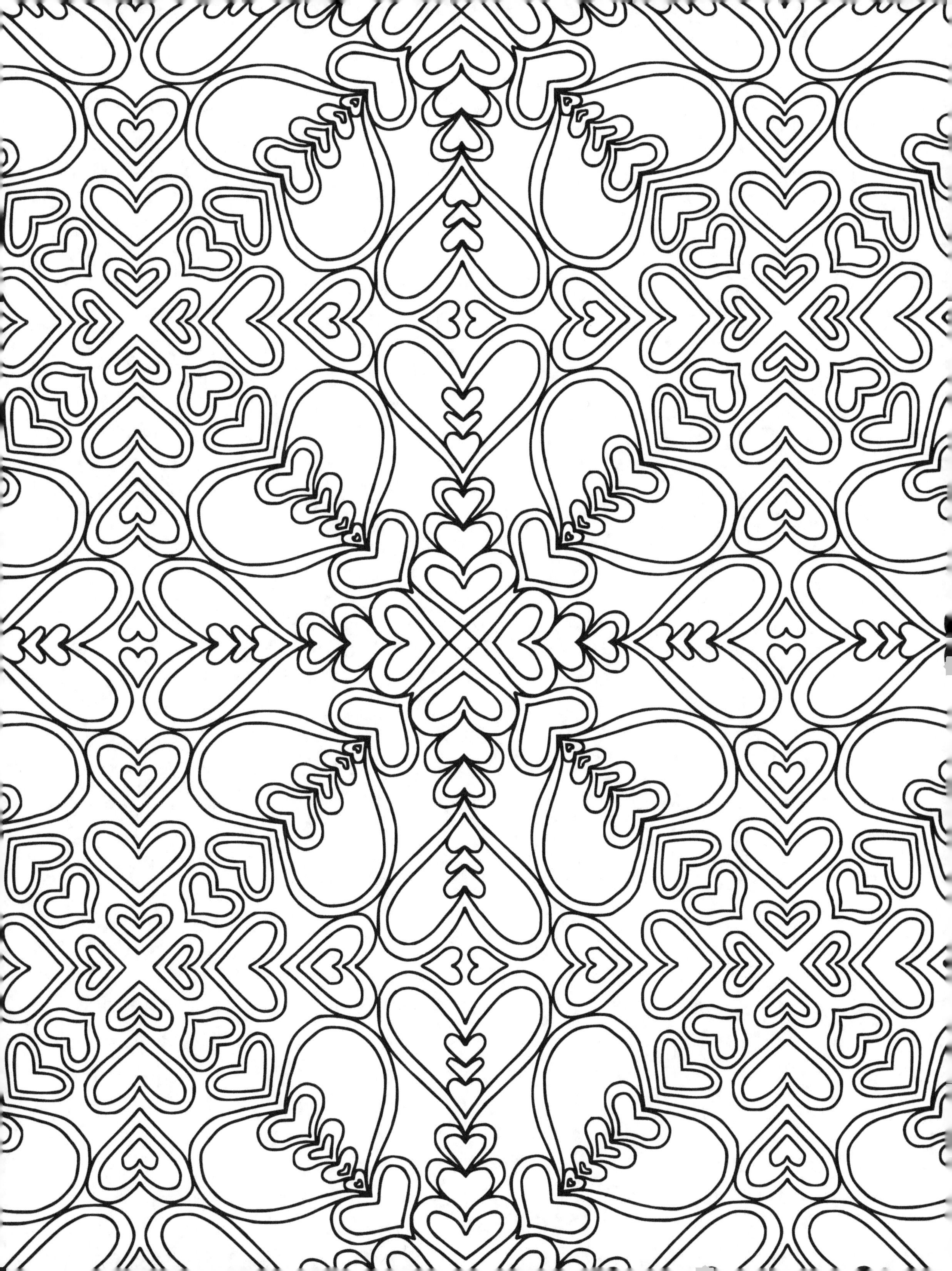

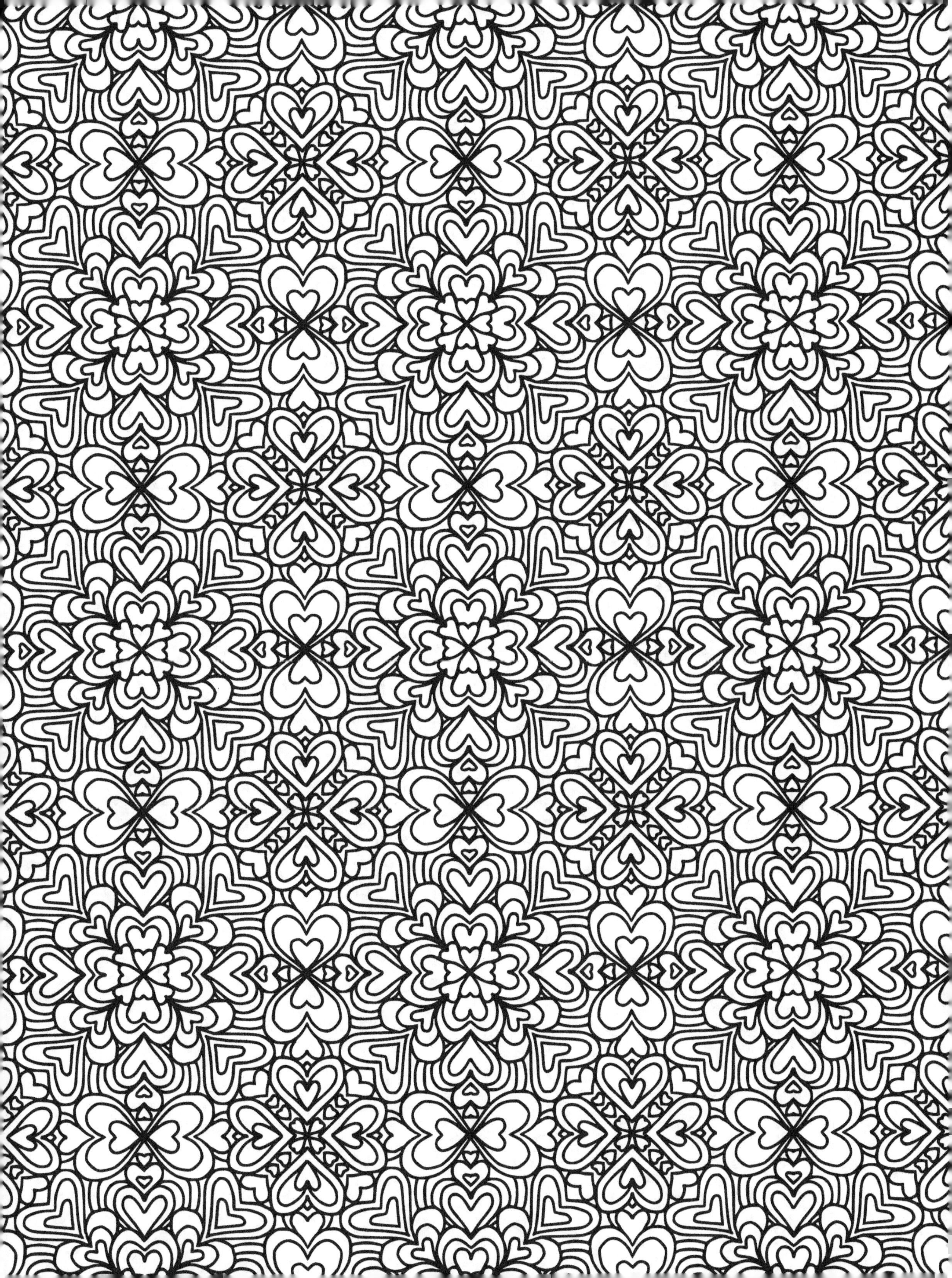

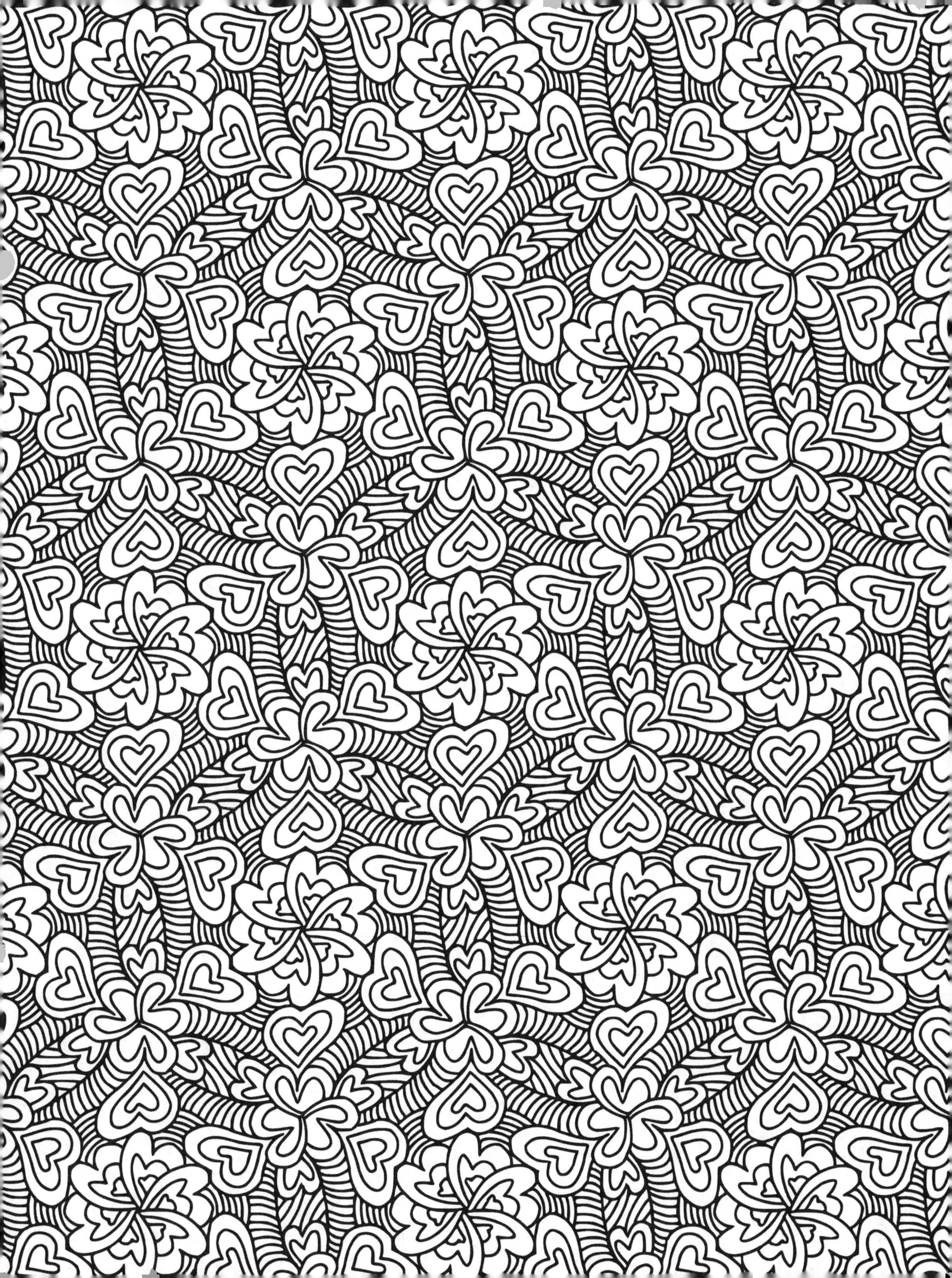

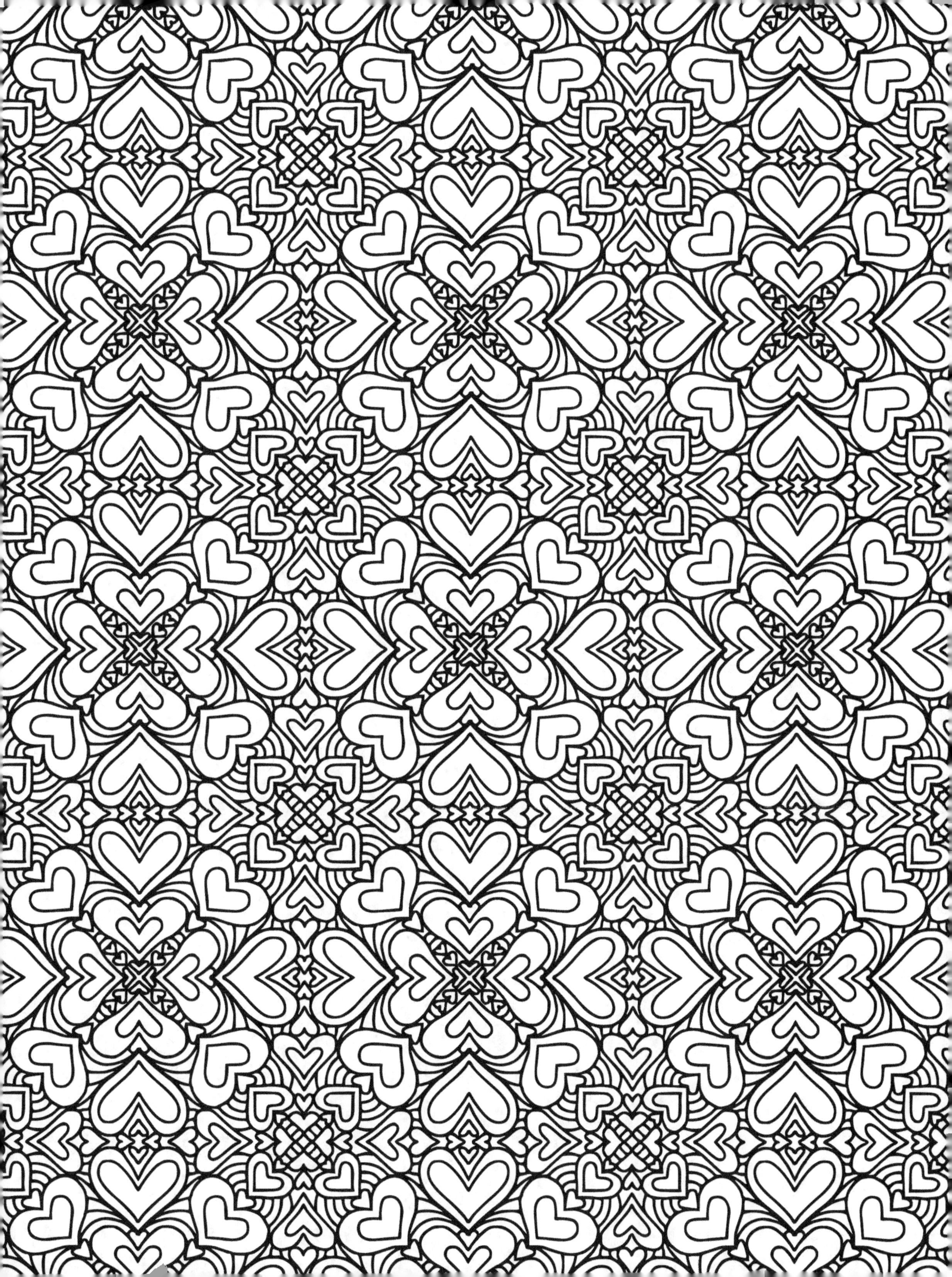

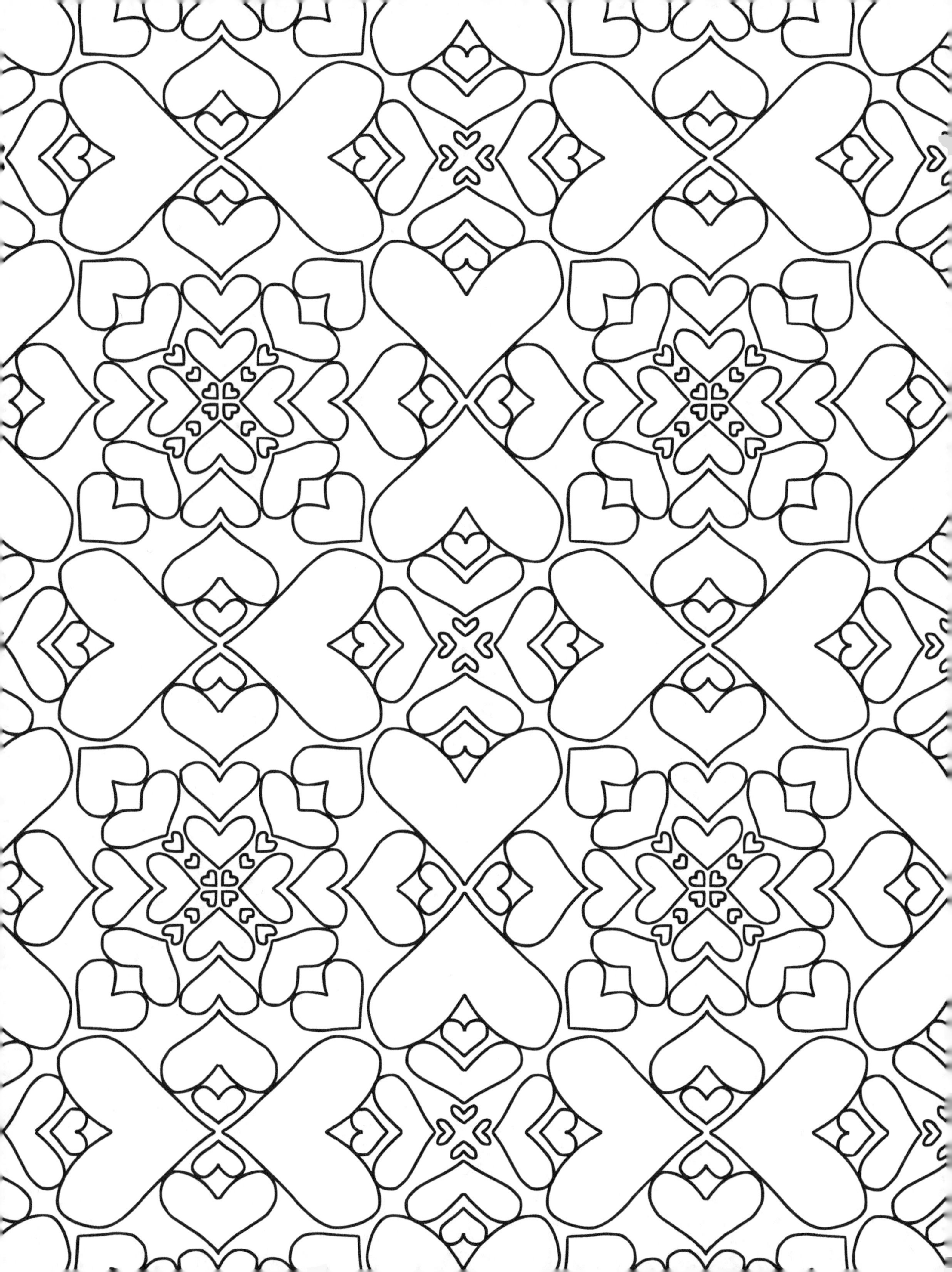

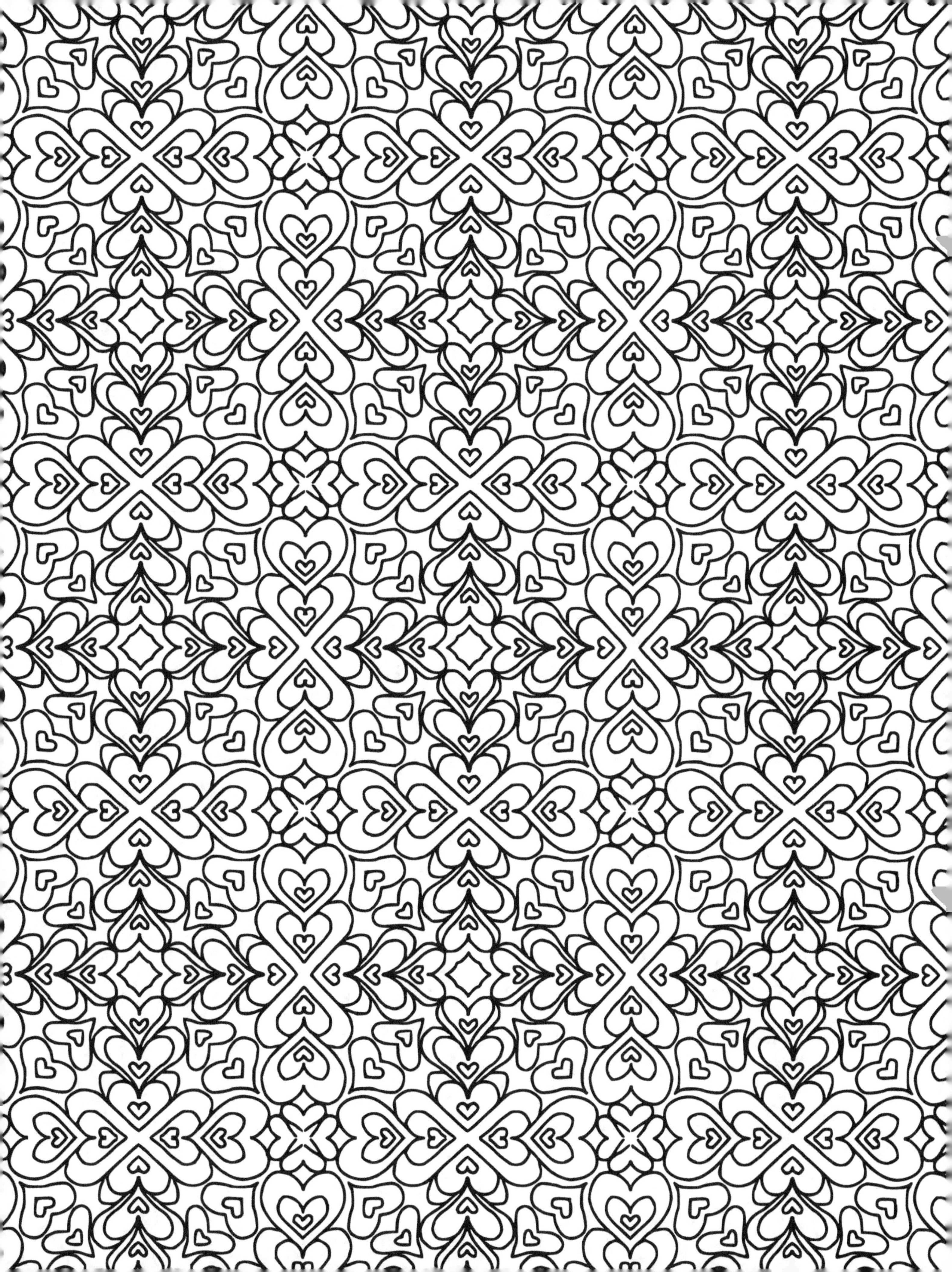

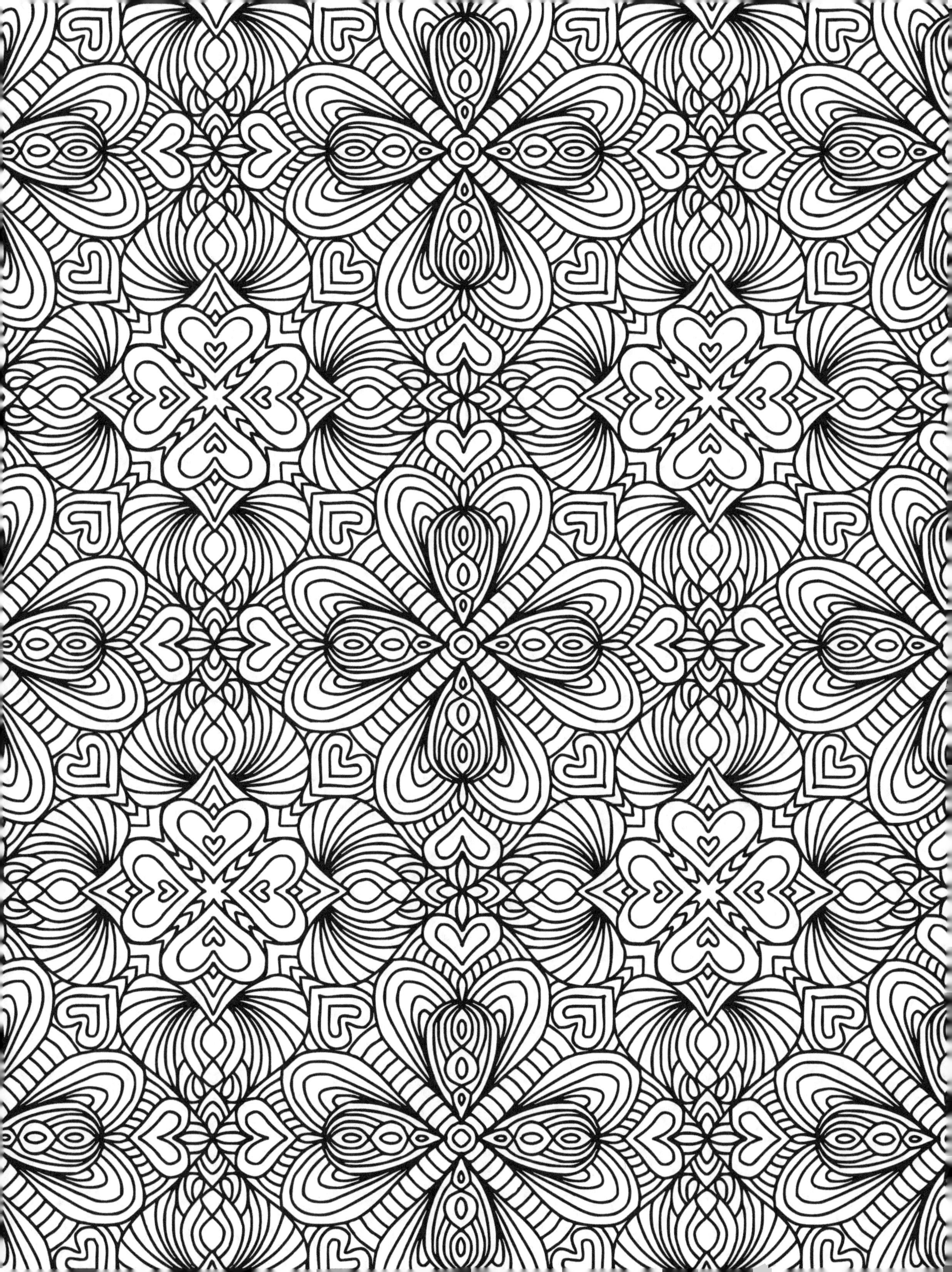

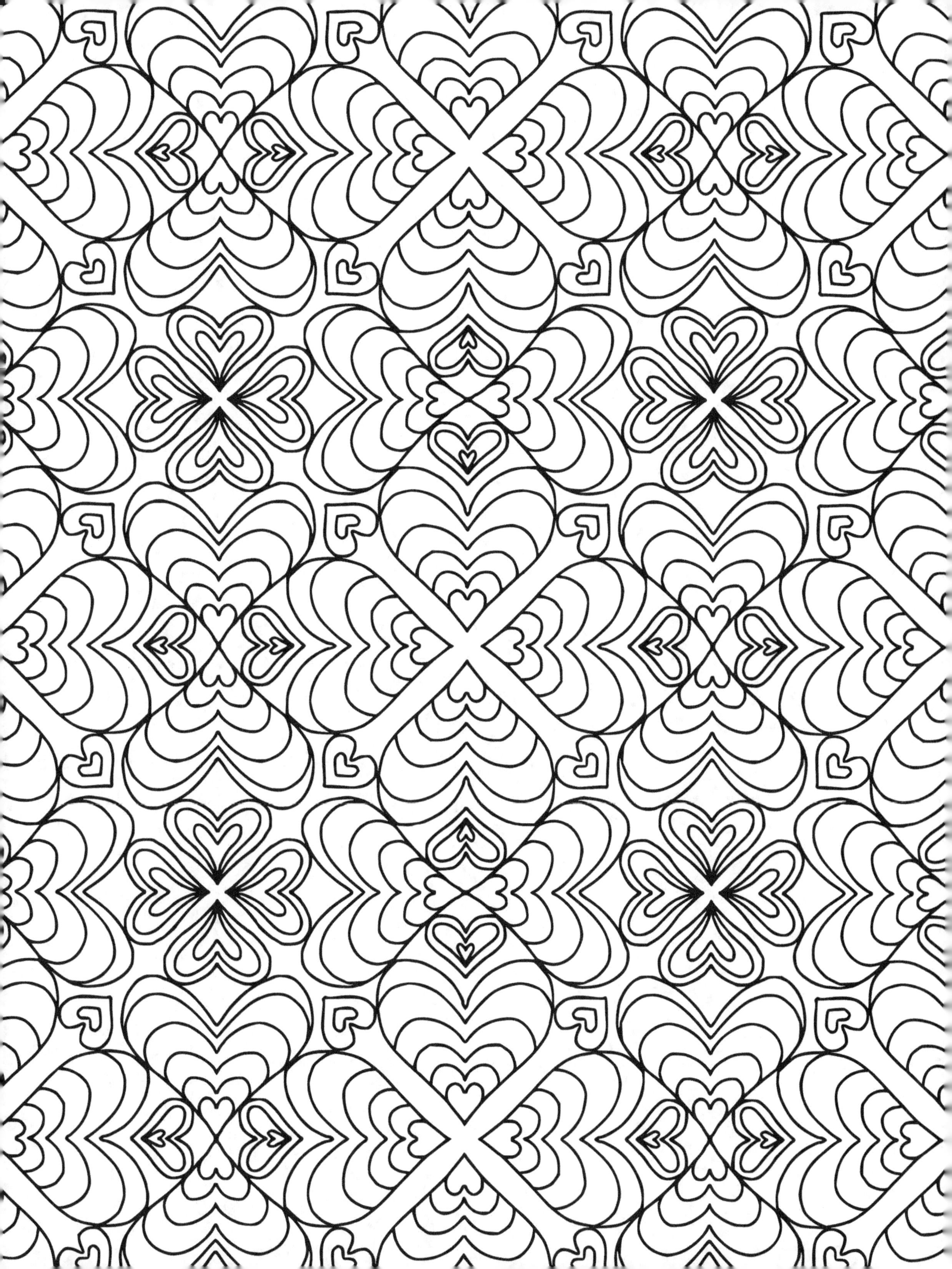

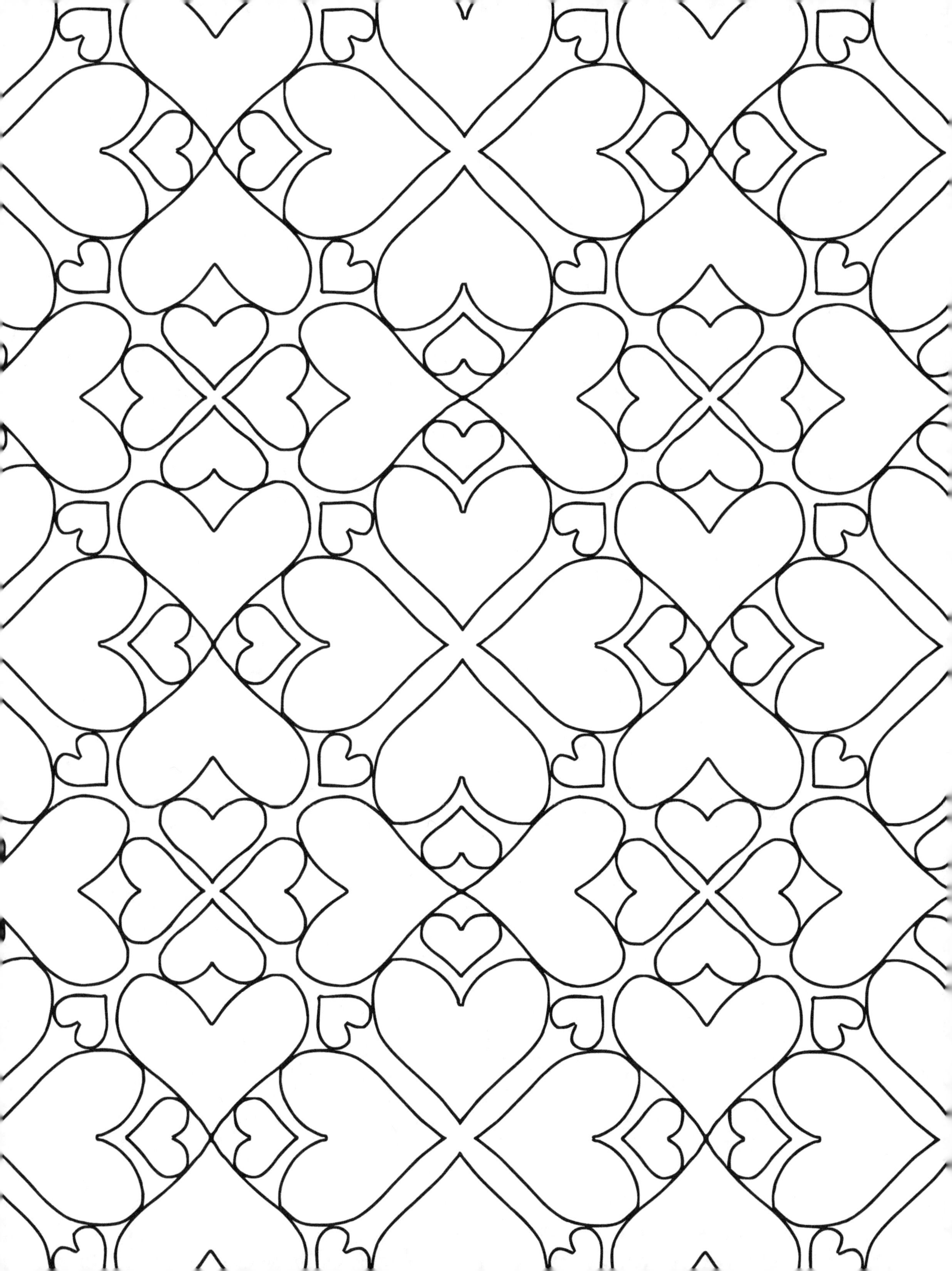

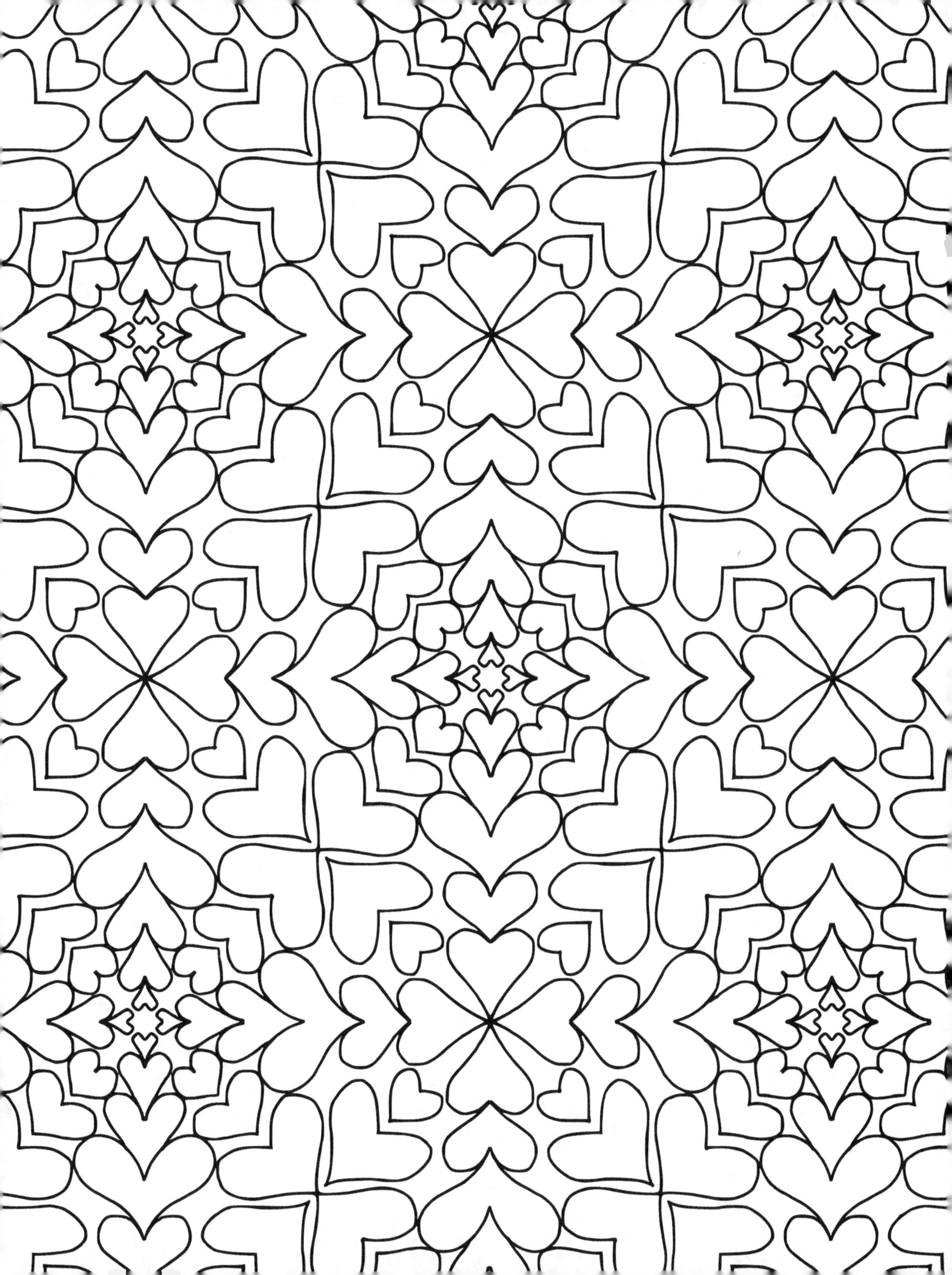

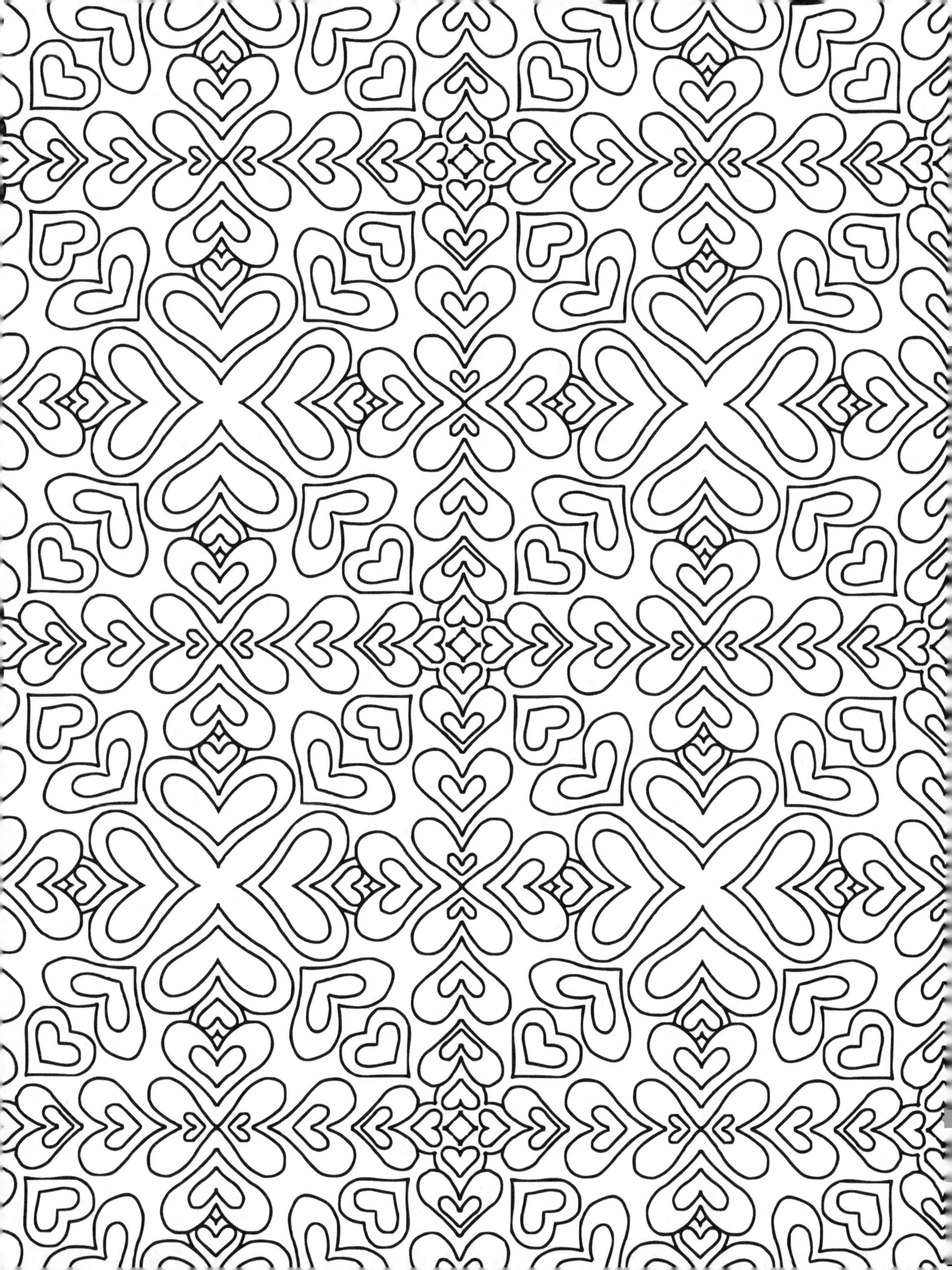

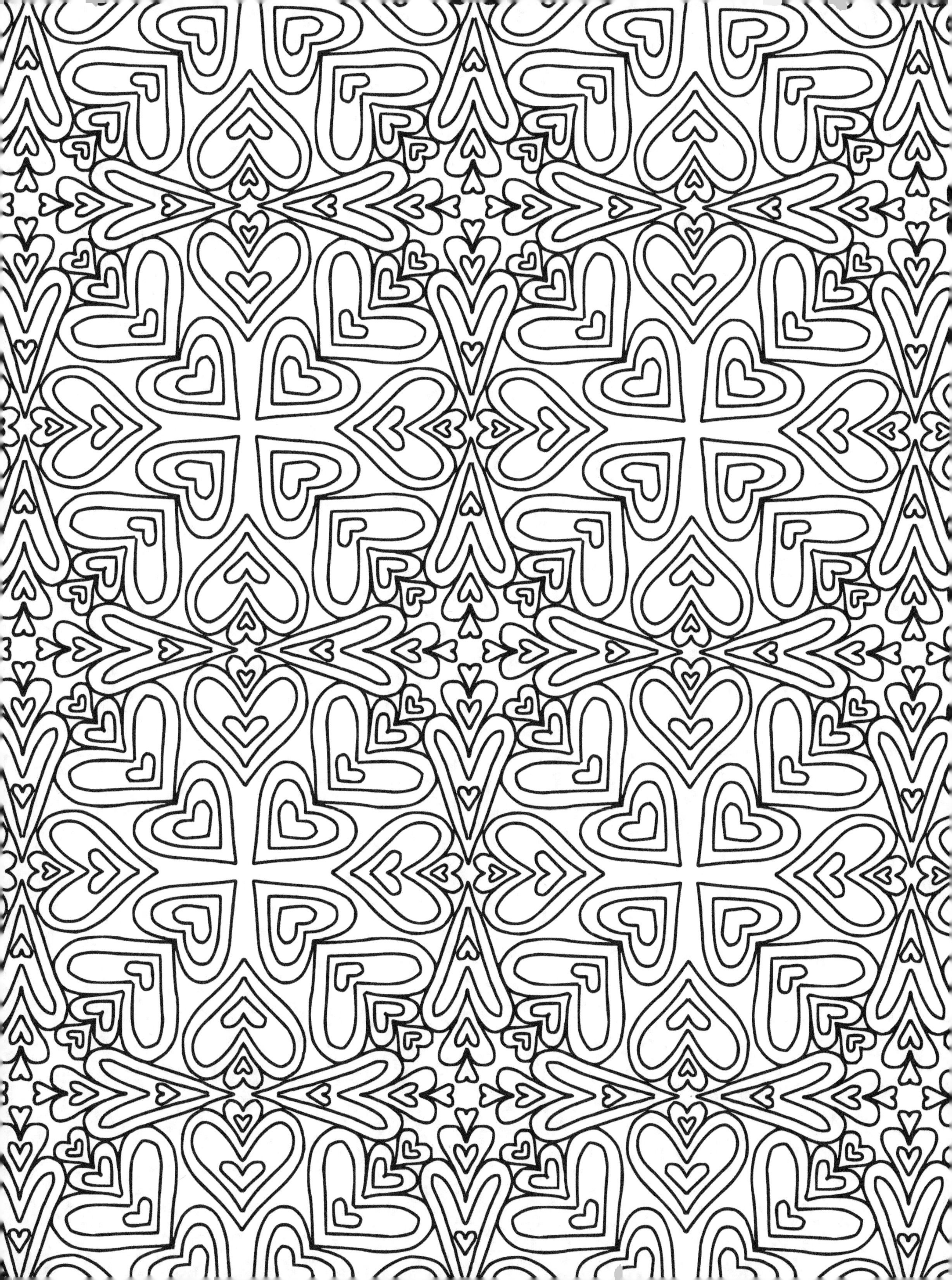

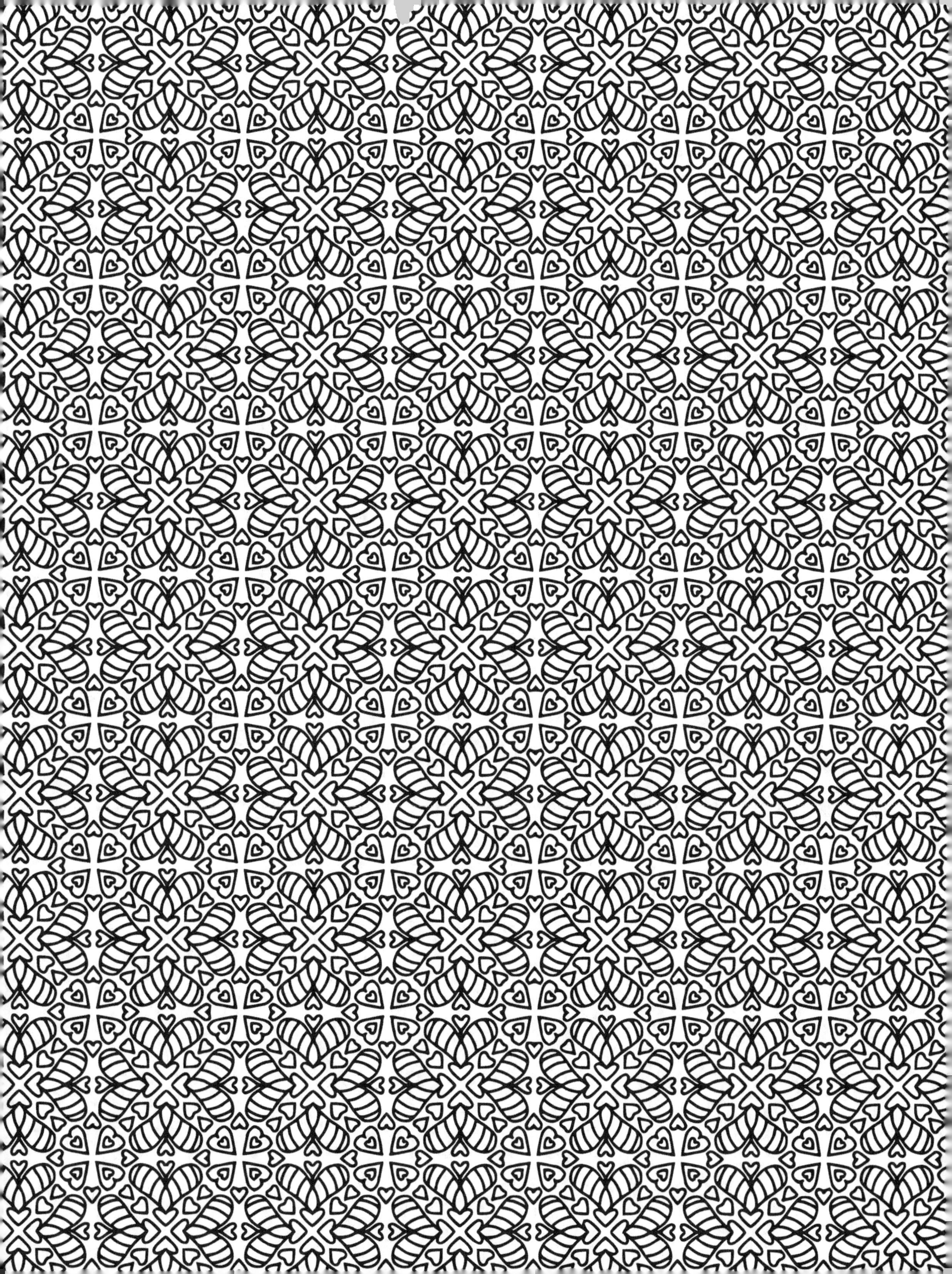

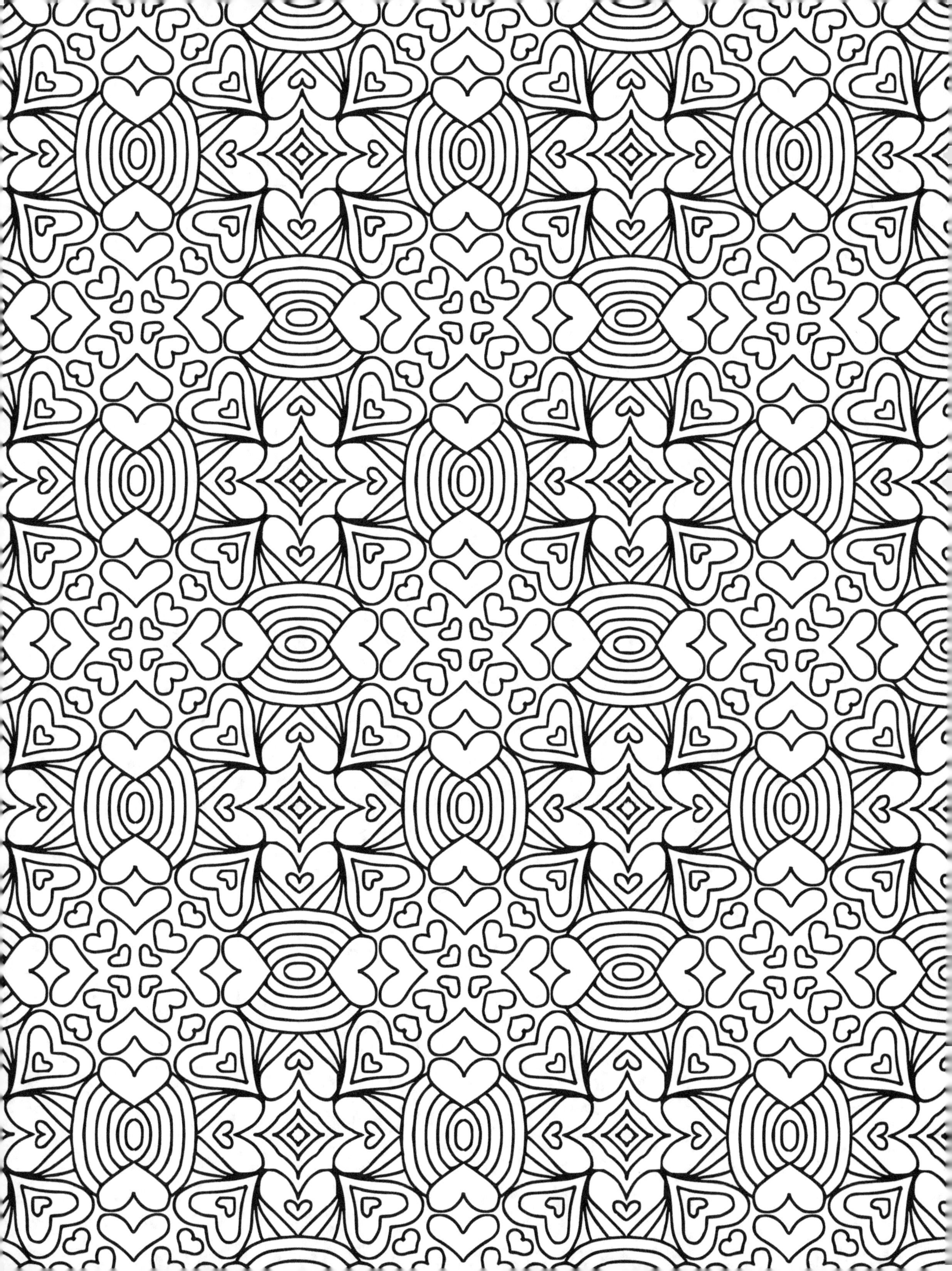

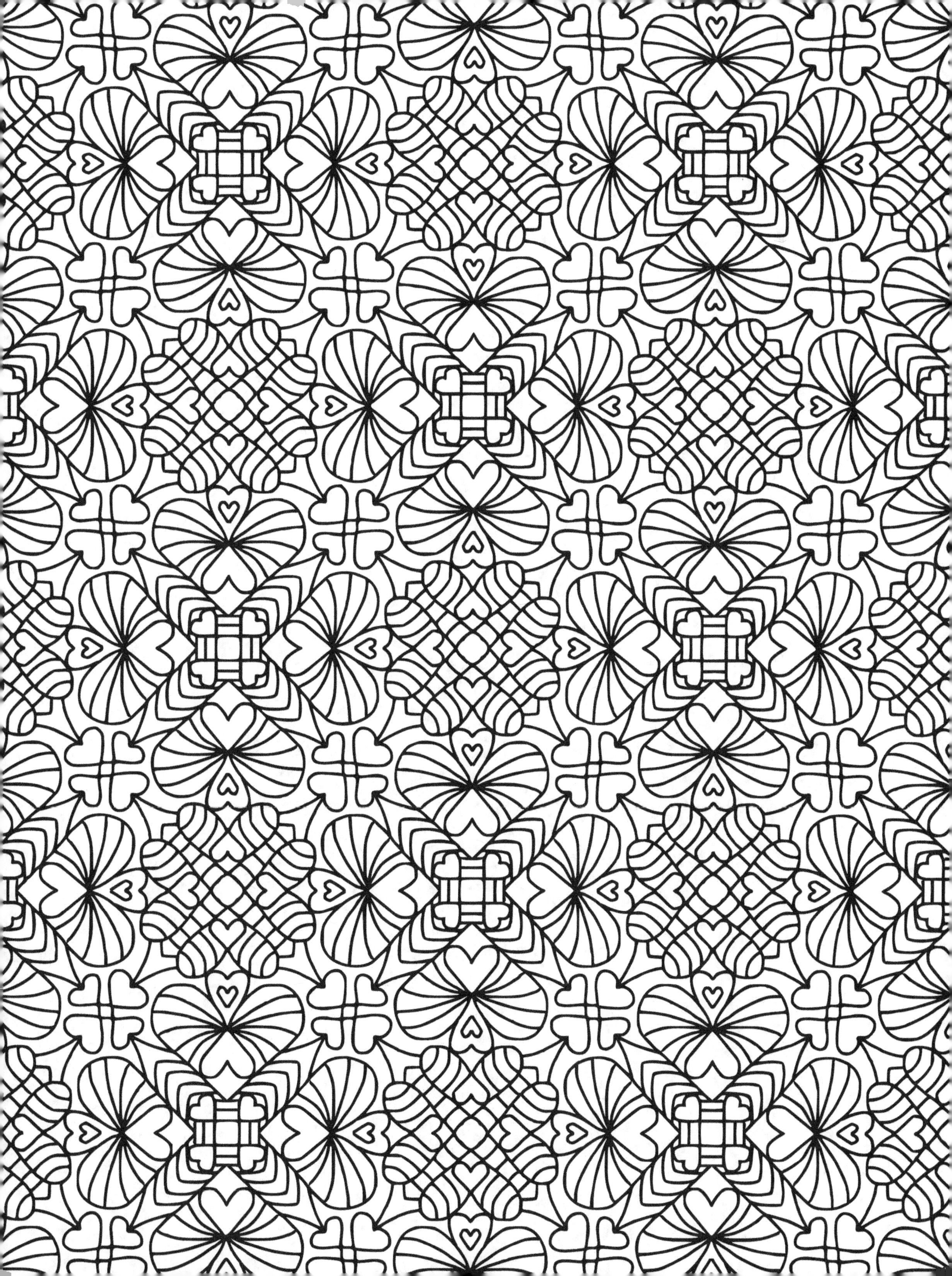

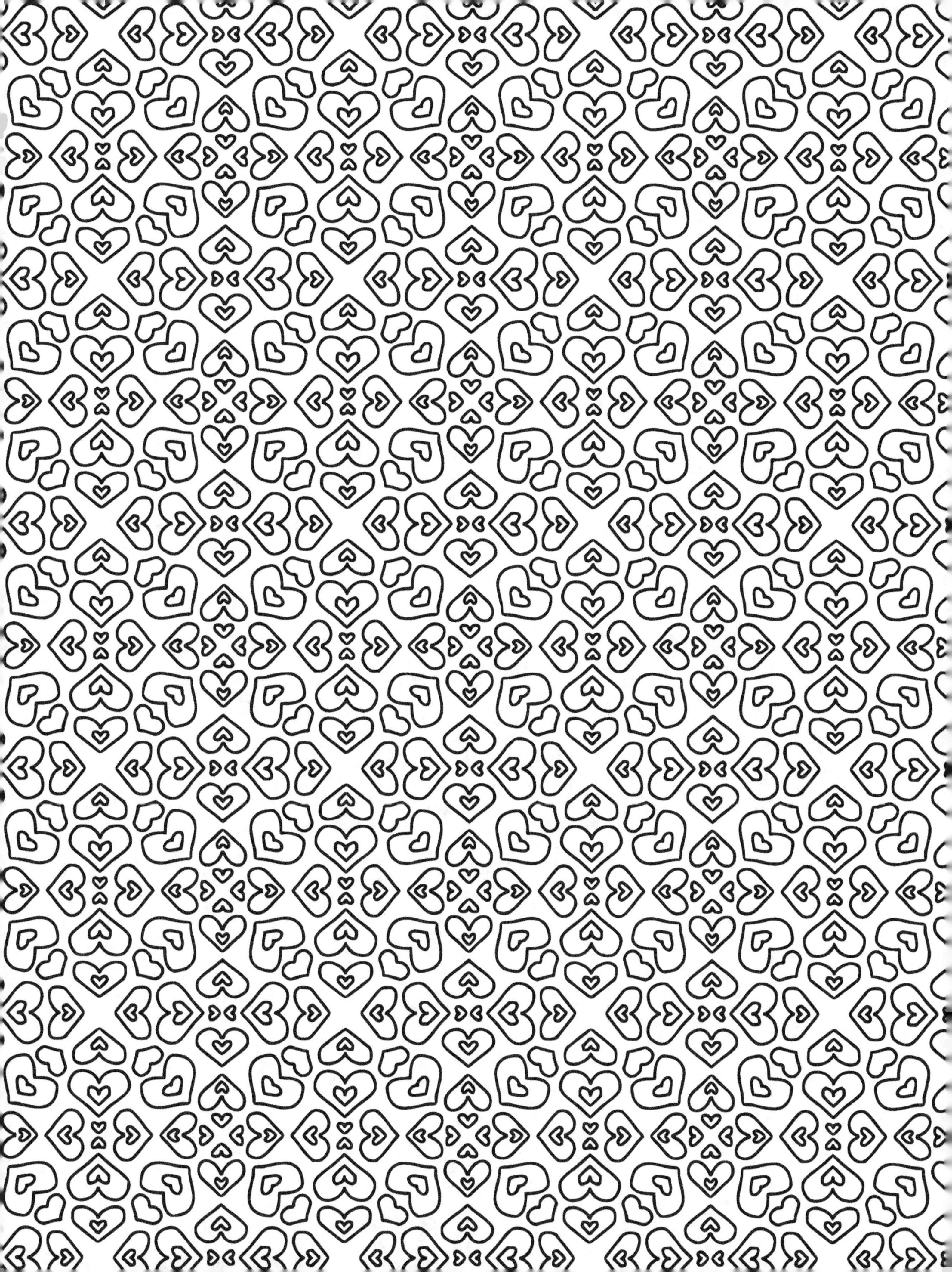

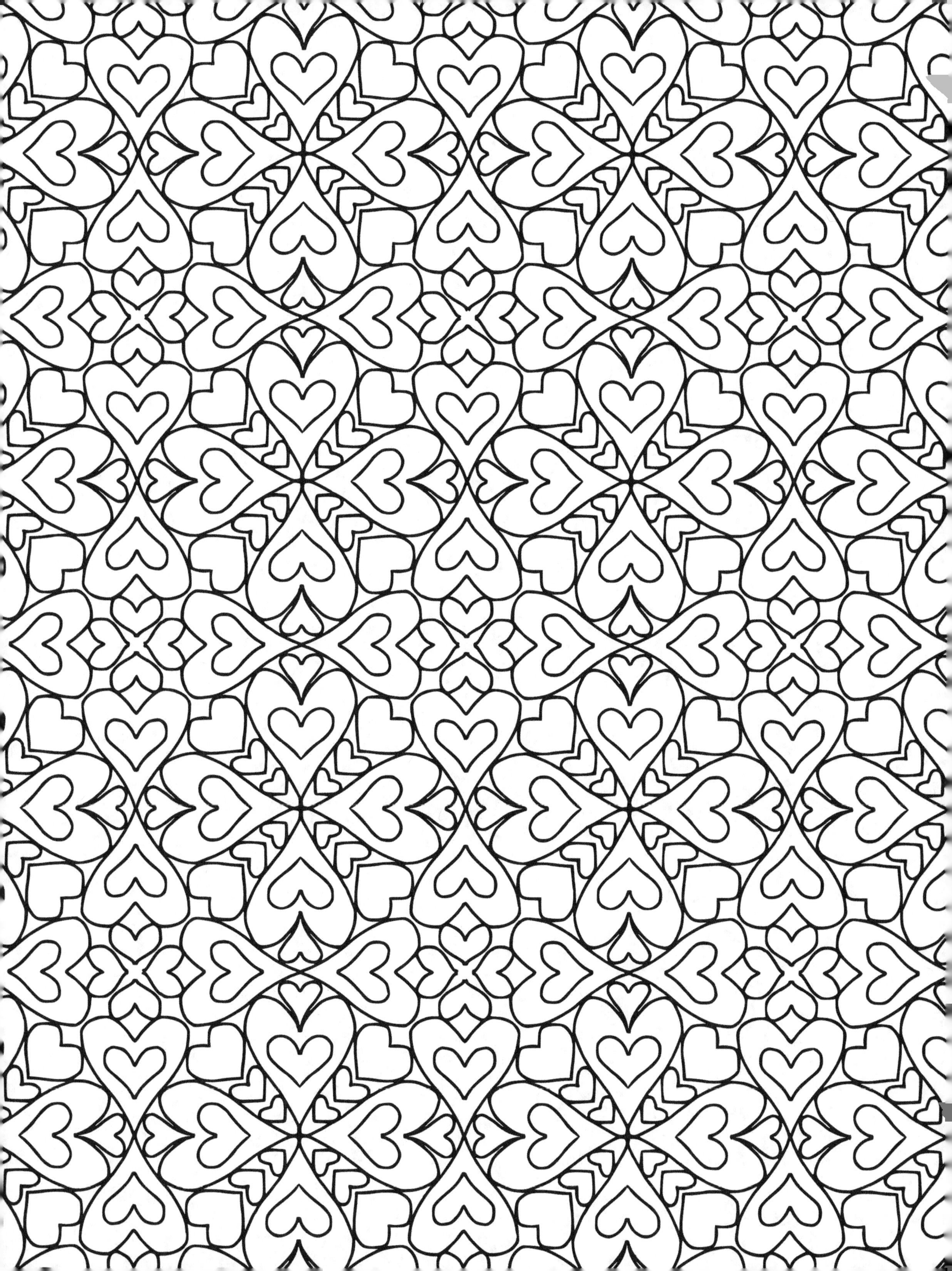

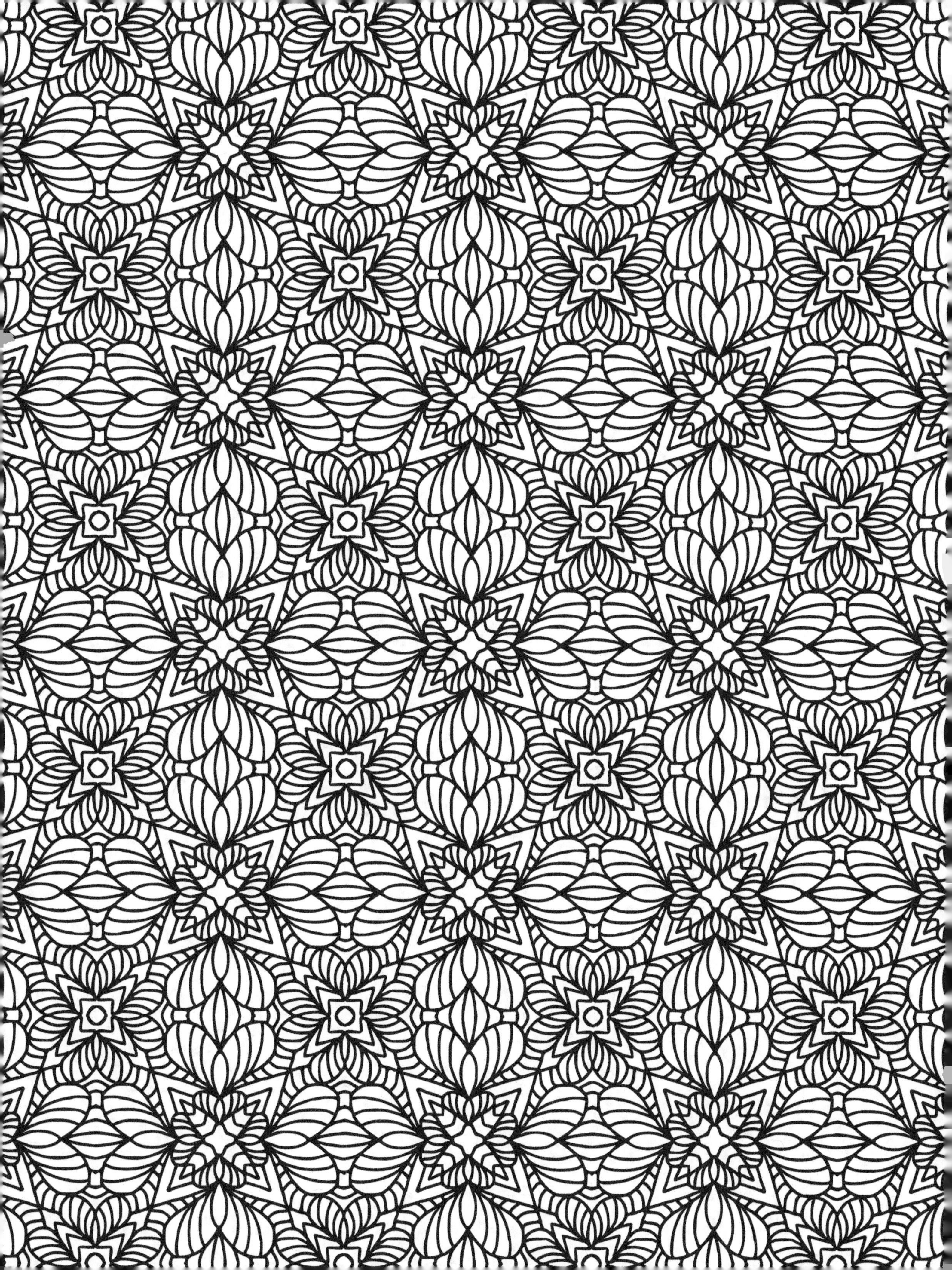

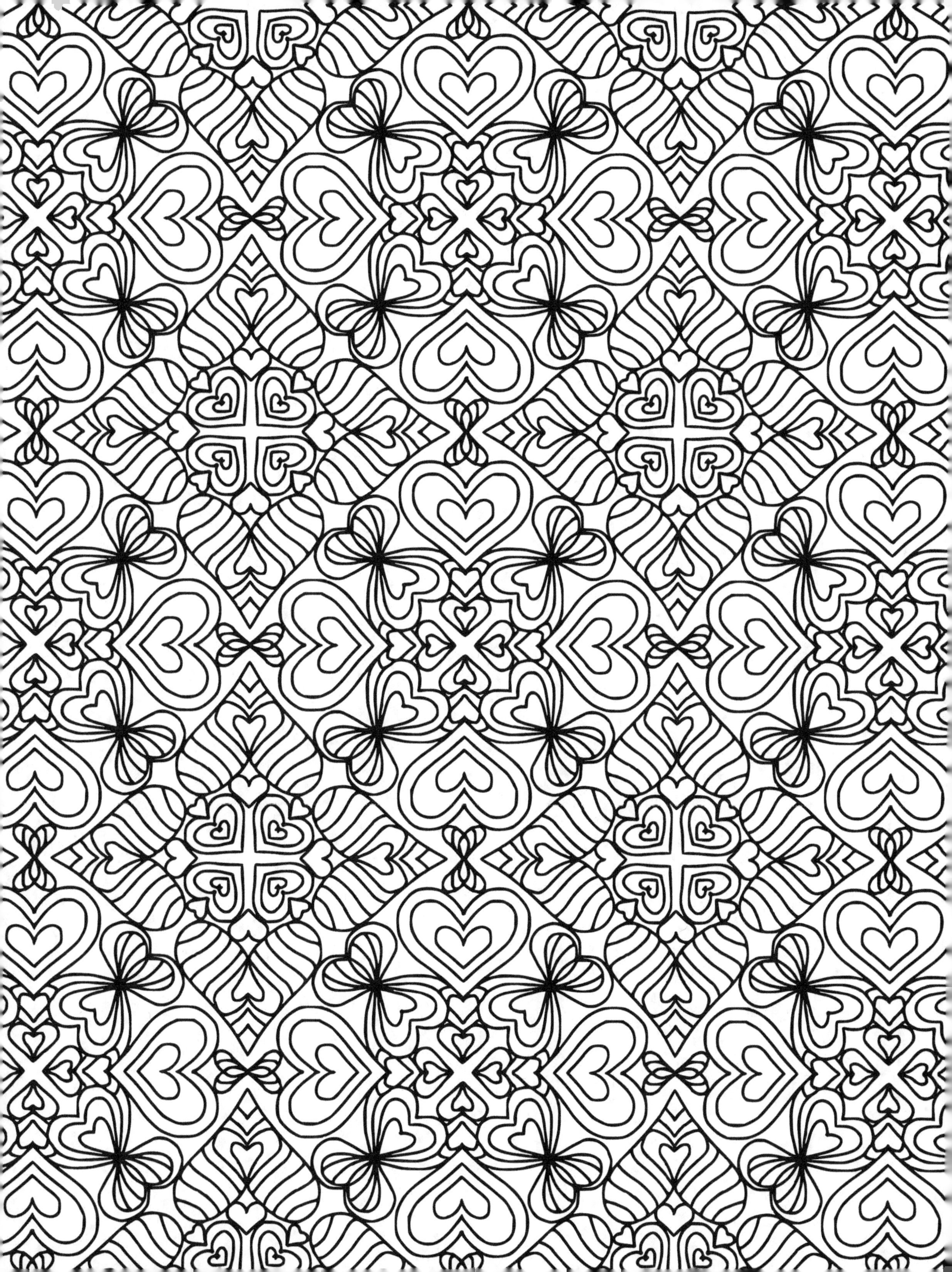

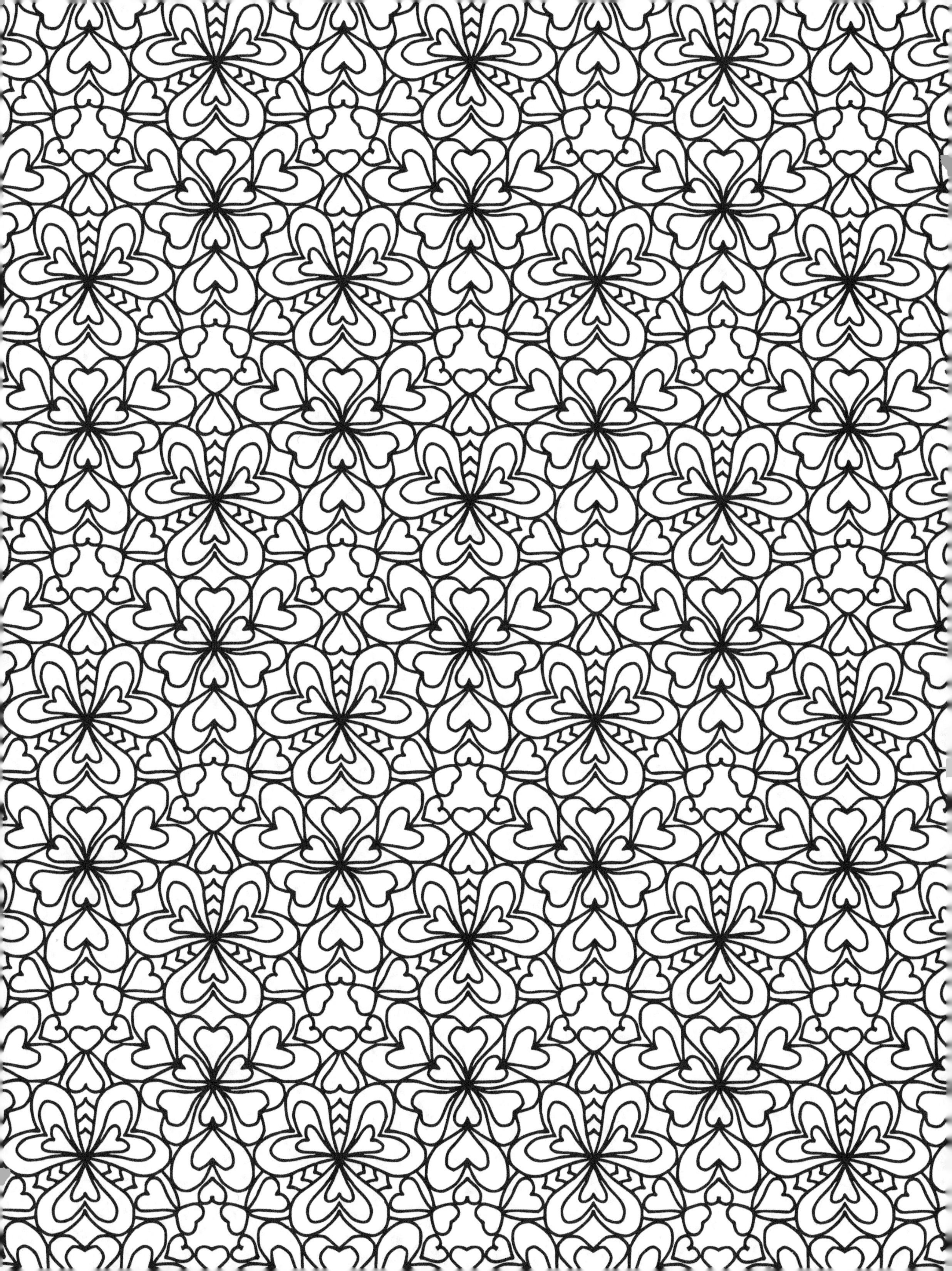

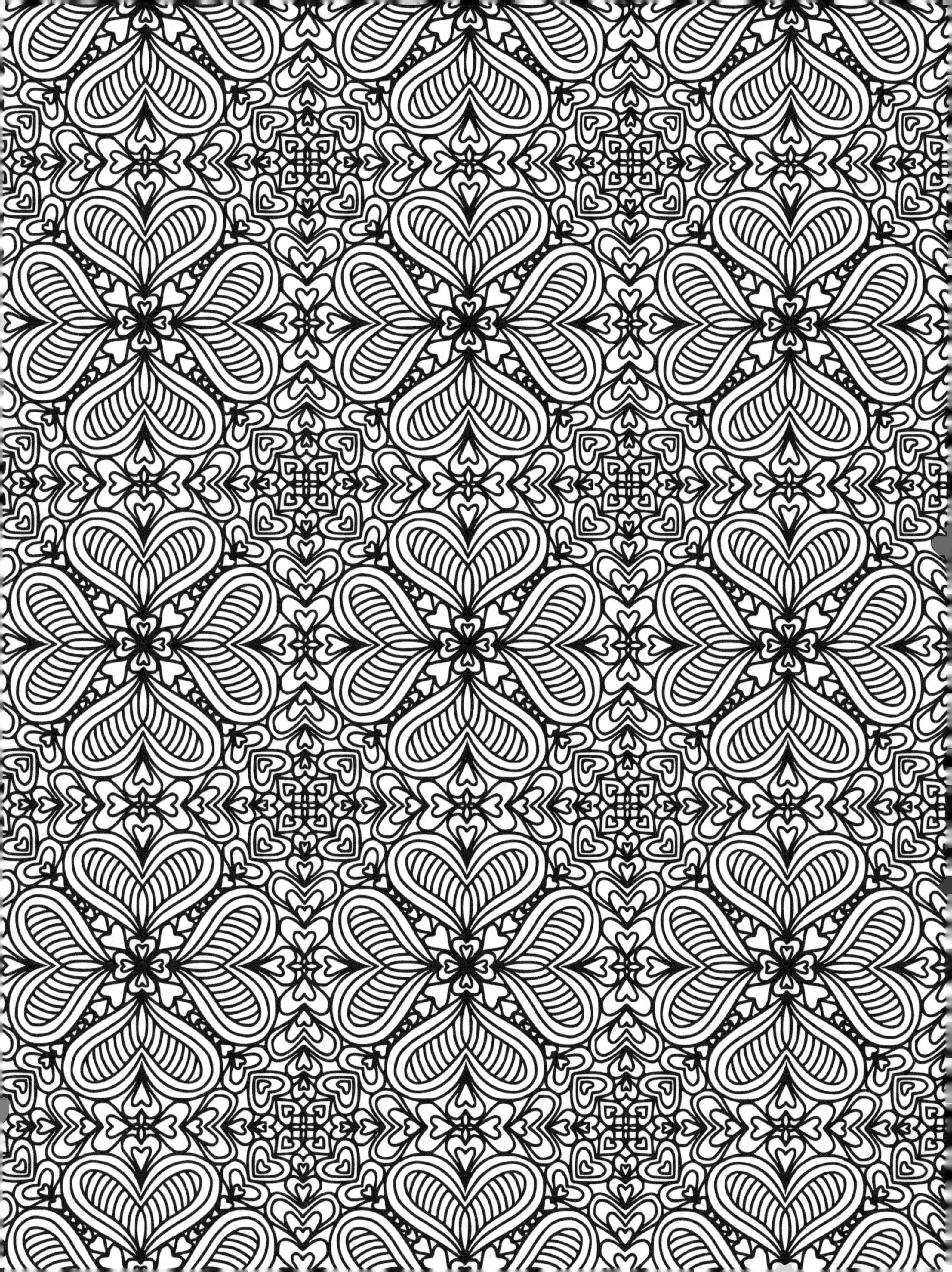

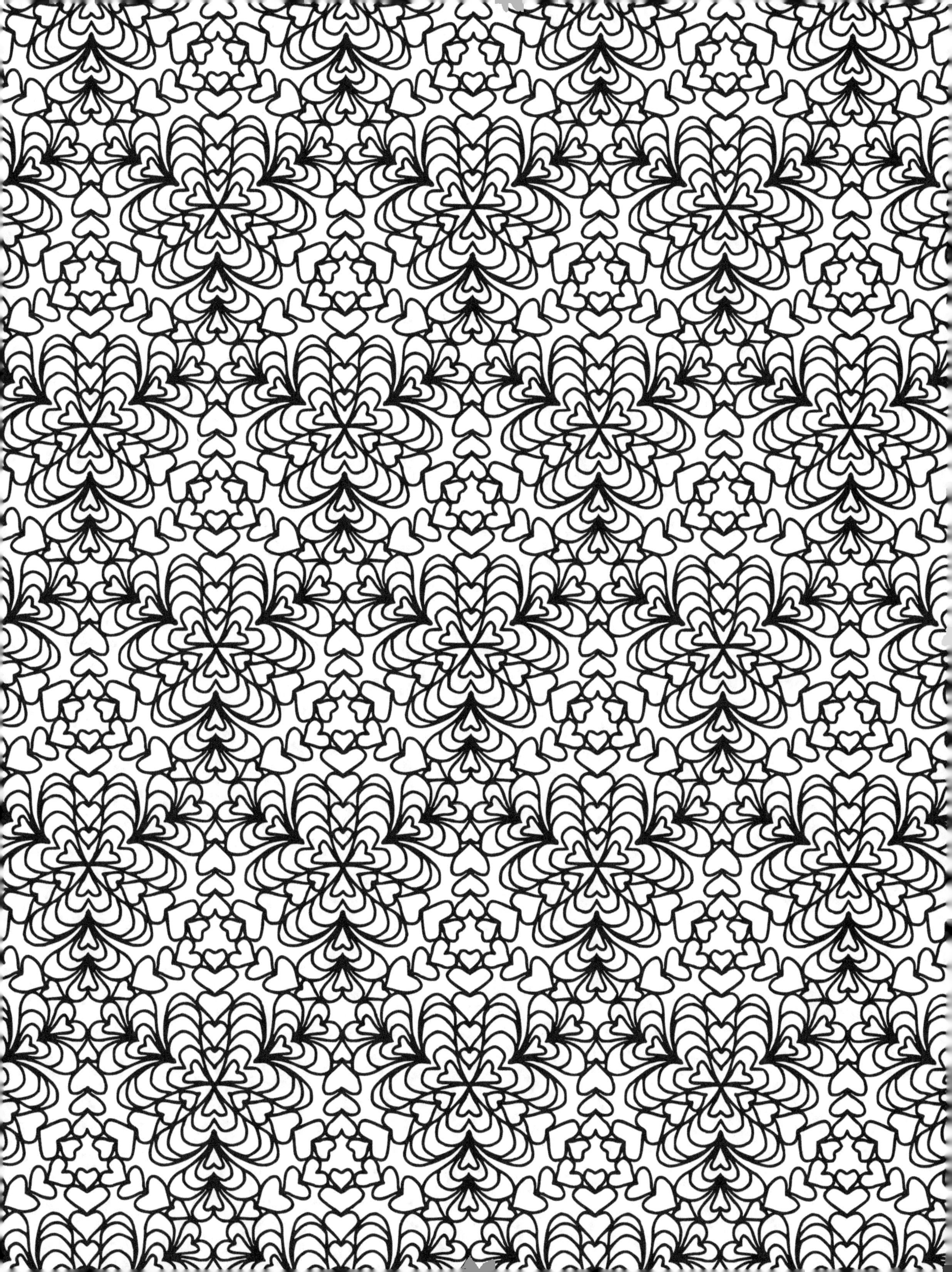

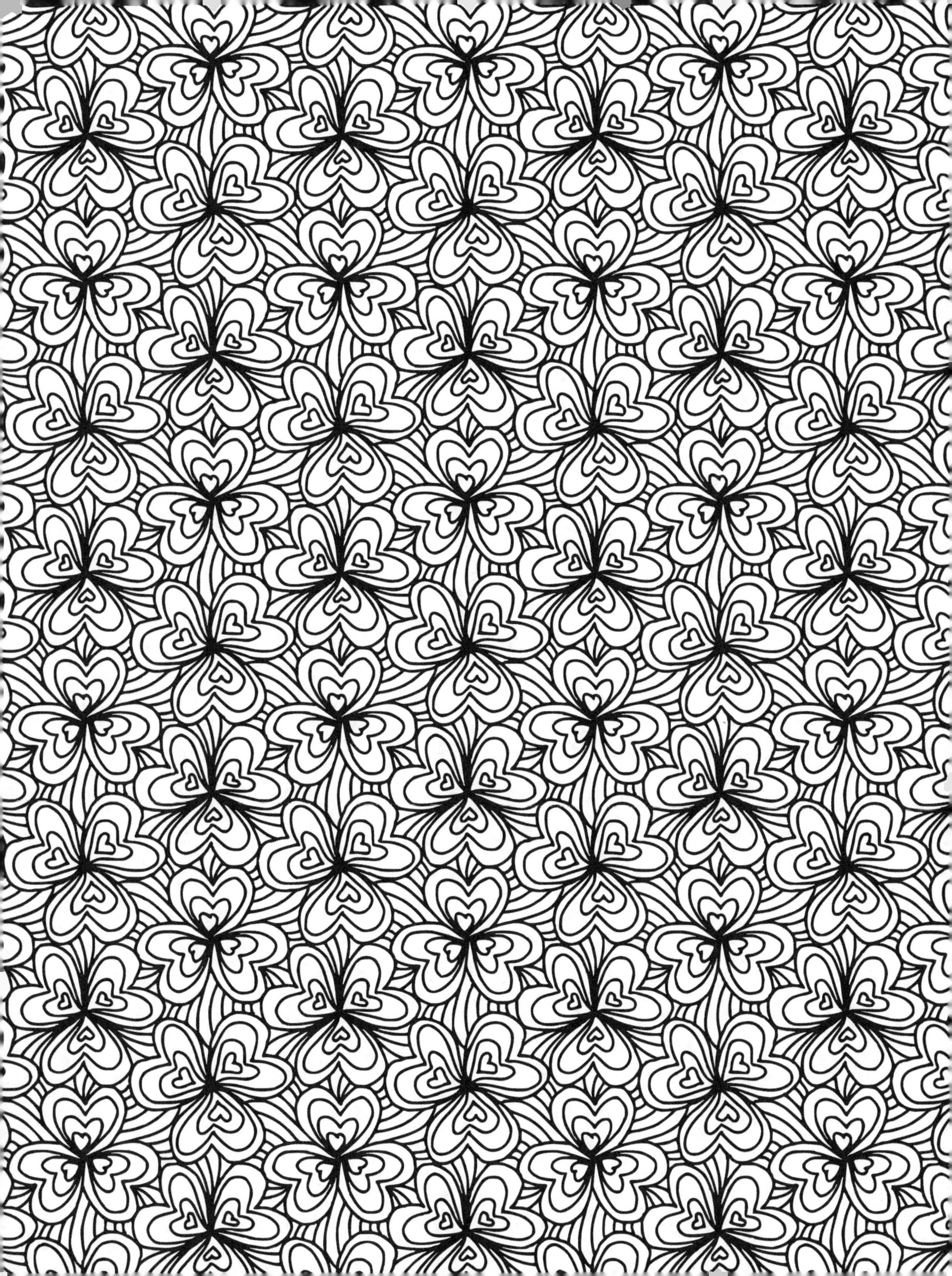

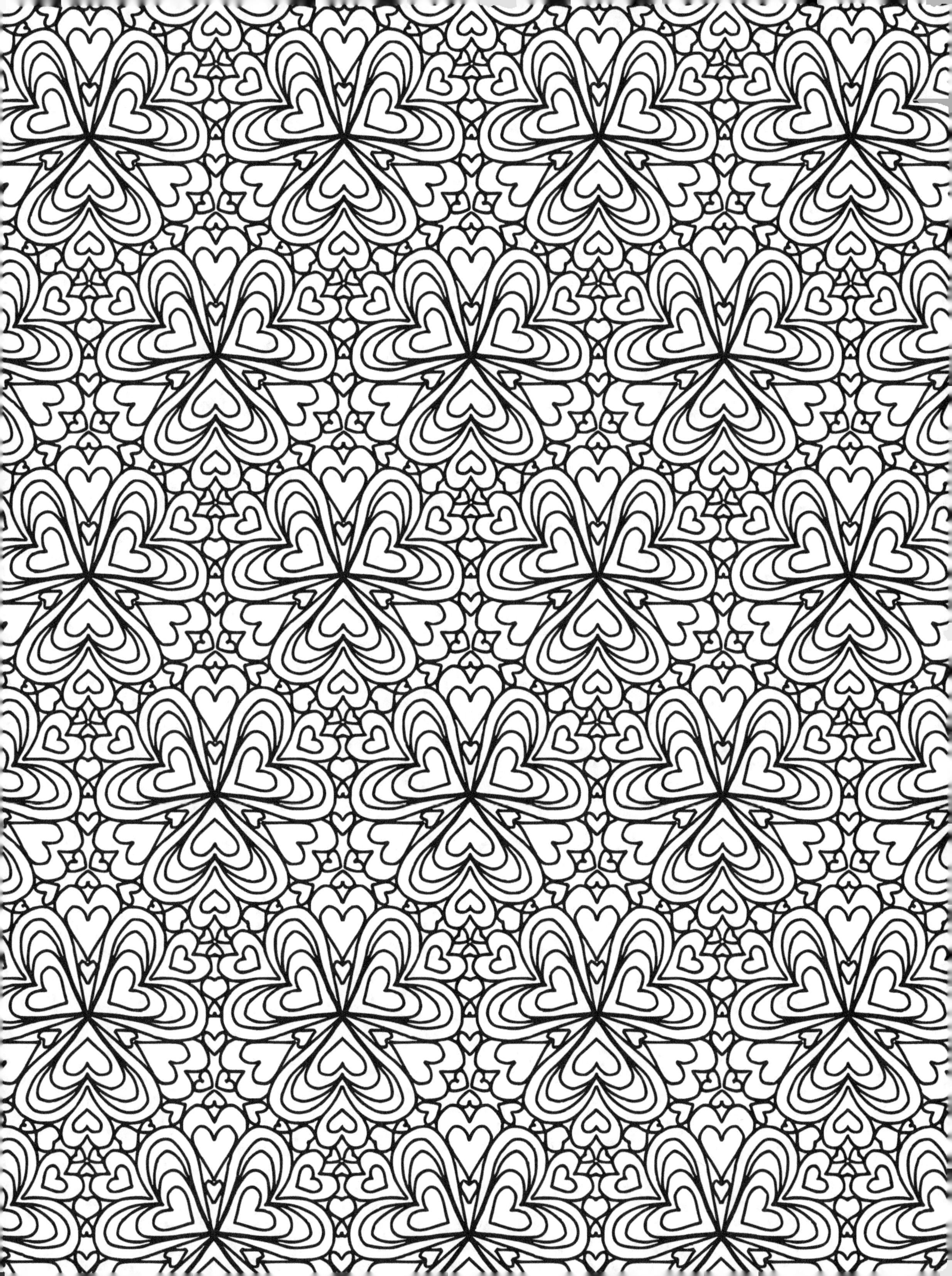

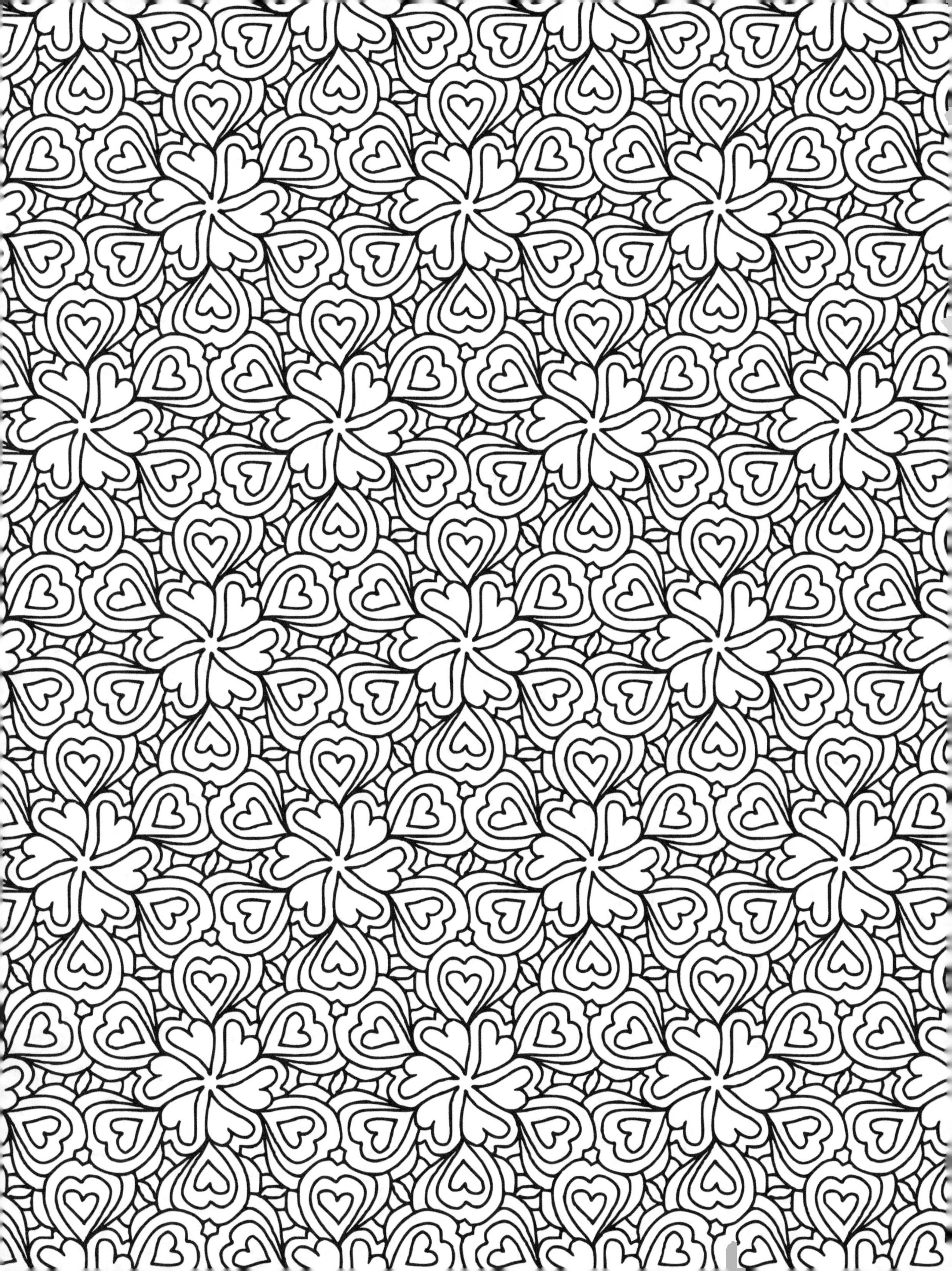

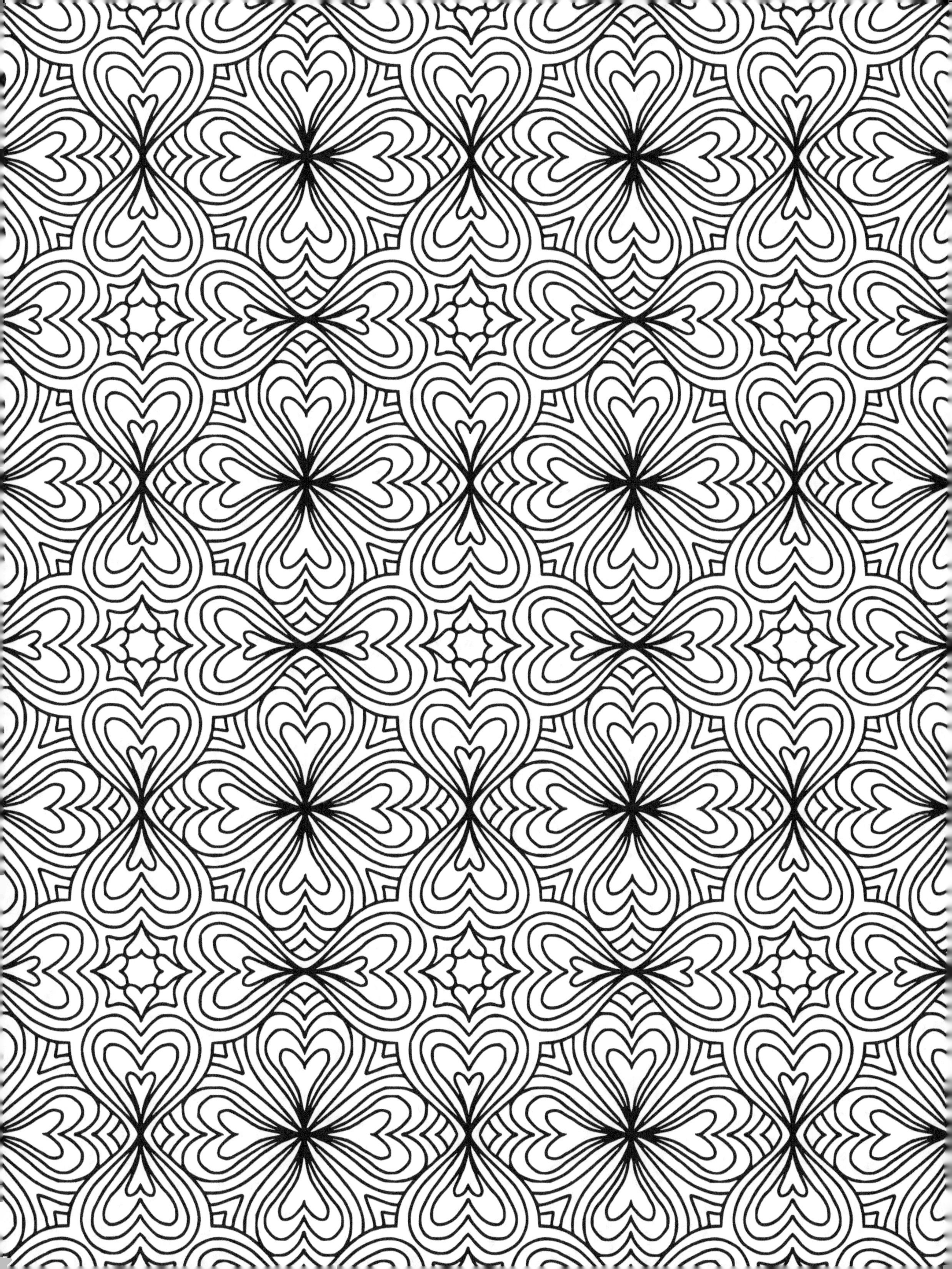

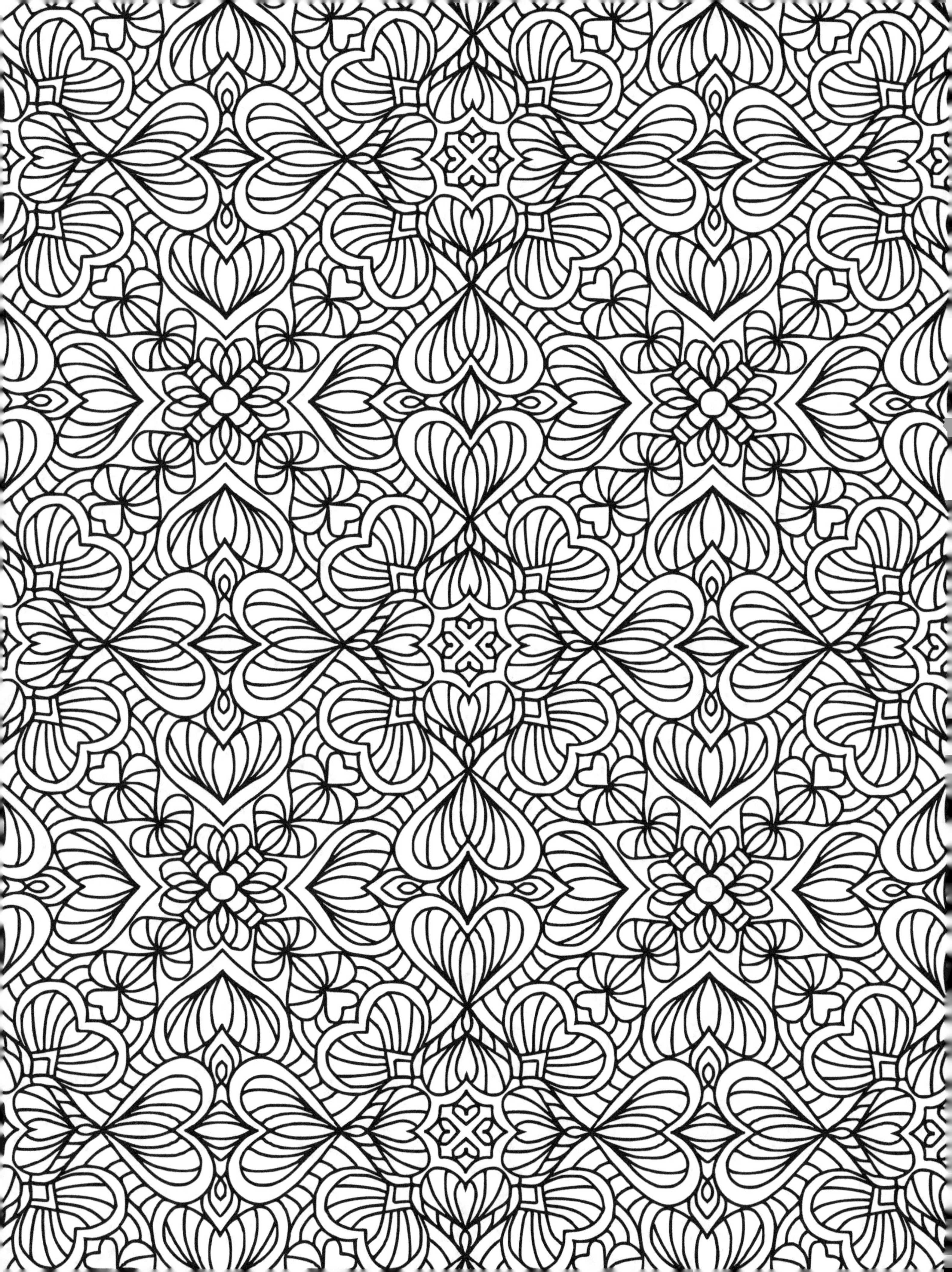

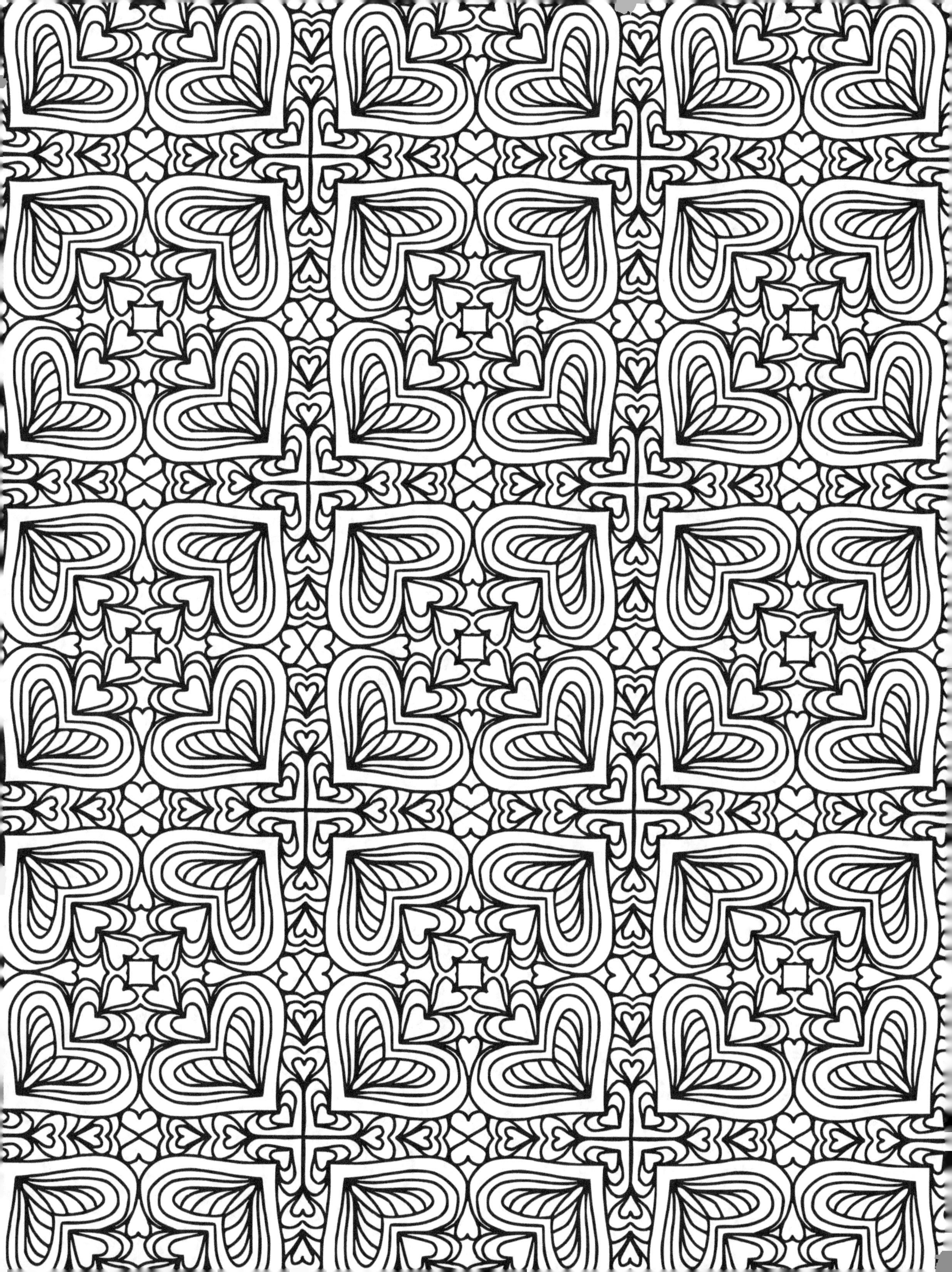

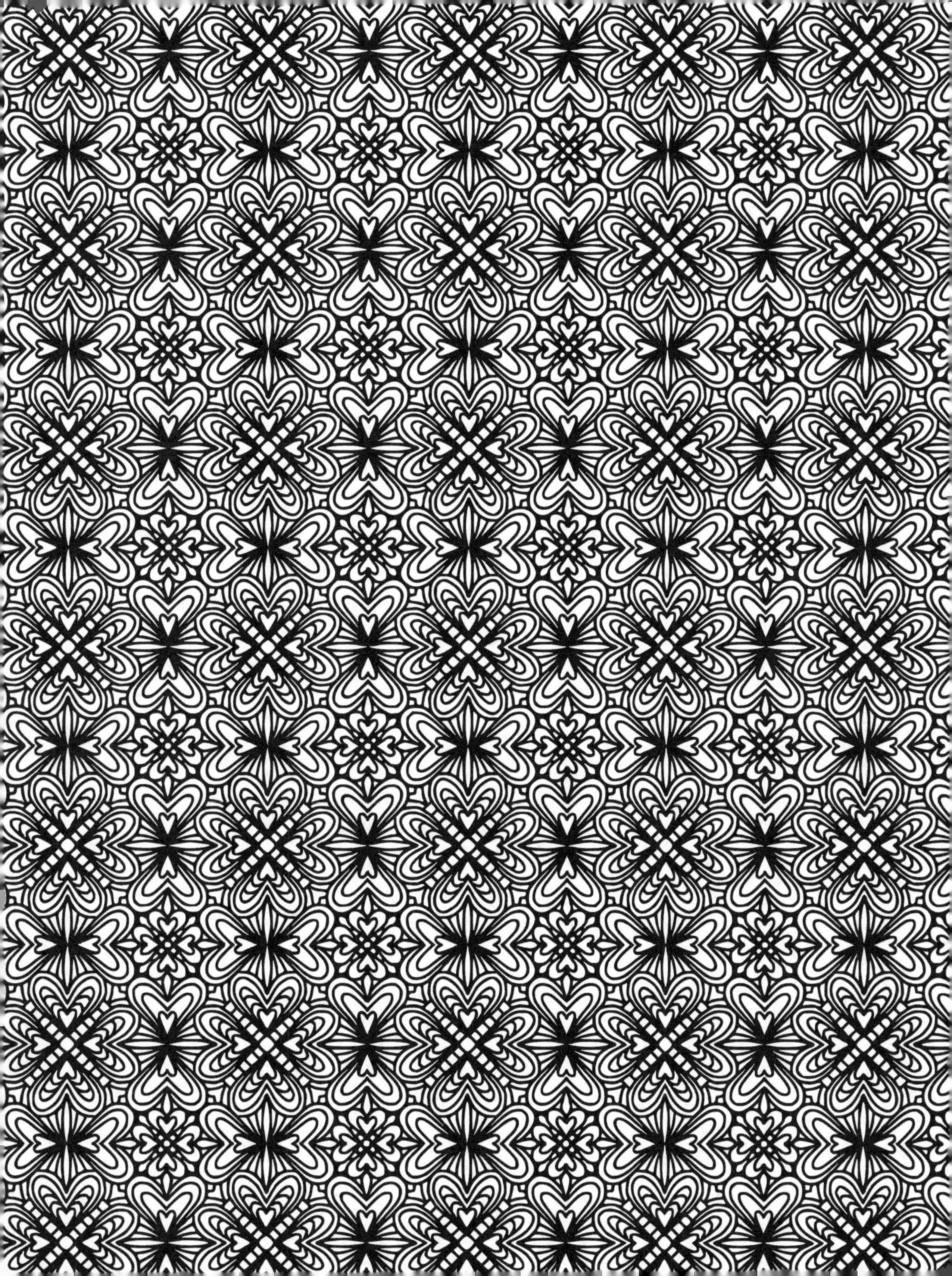

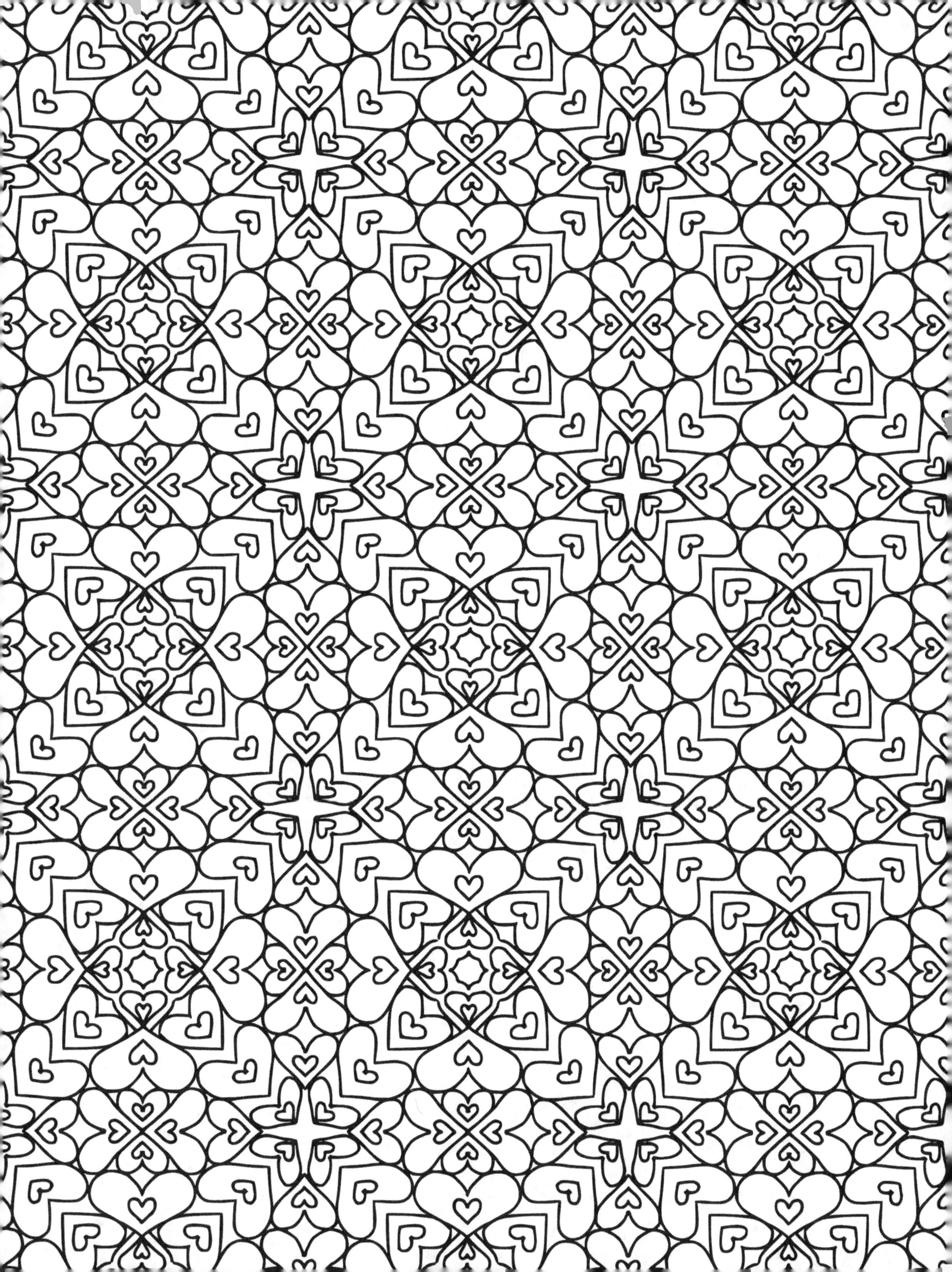

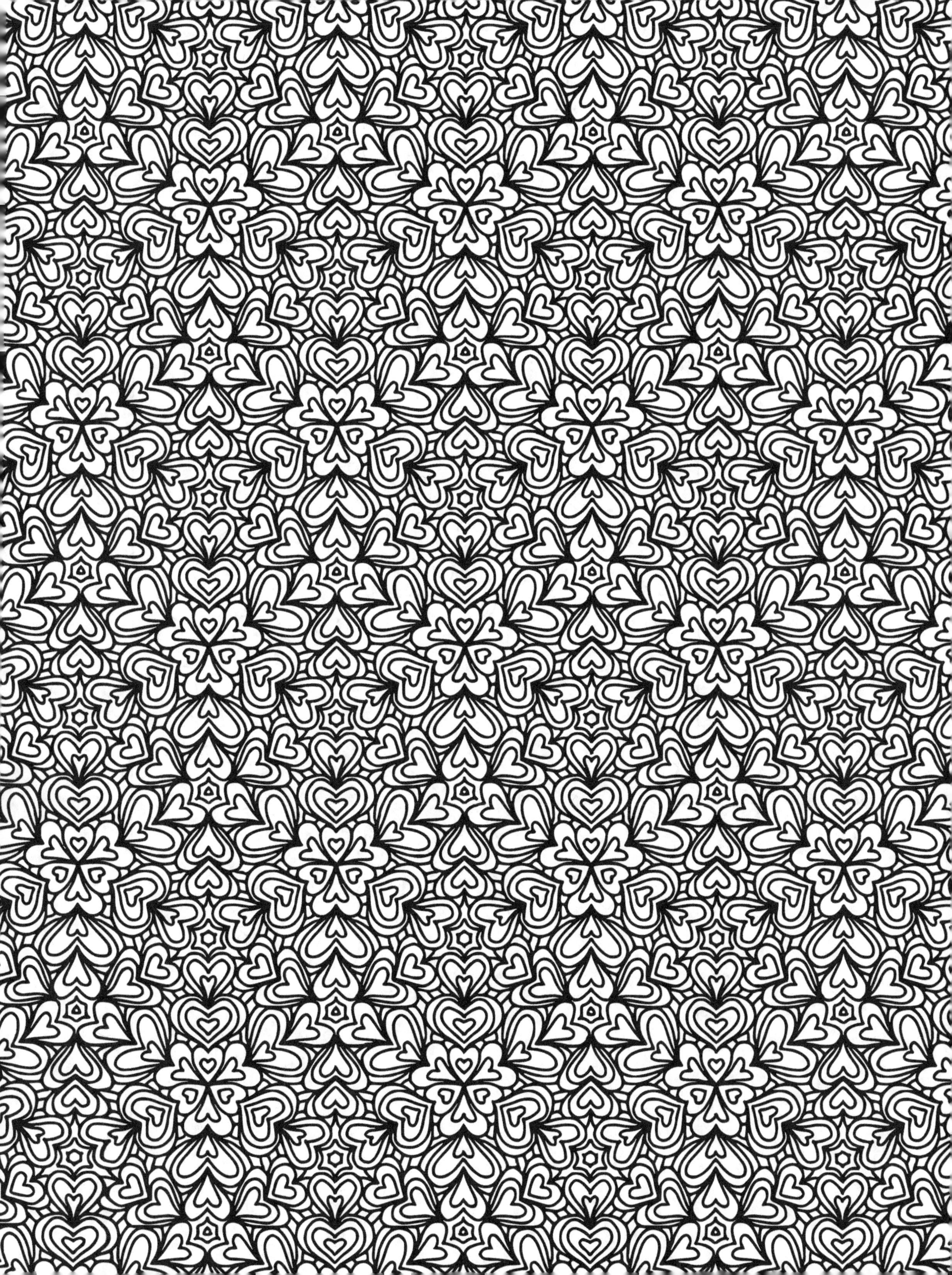

Test your colors here on the samples from
"My Pocket Coloring Companion"
&
"My Coloring Companion"

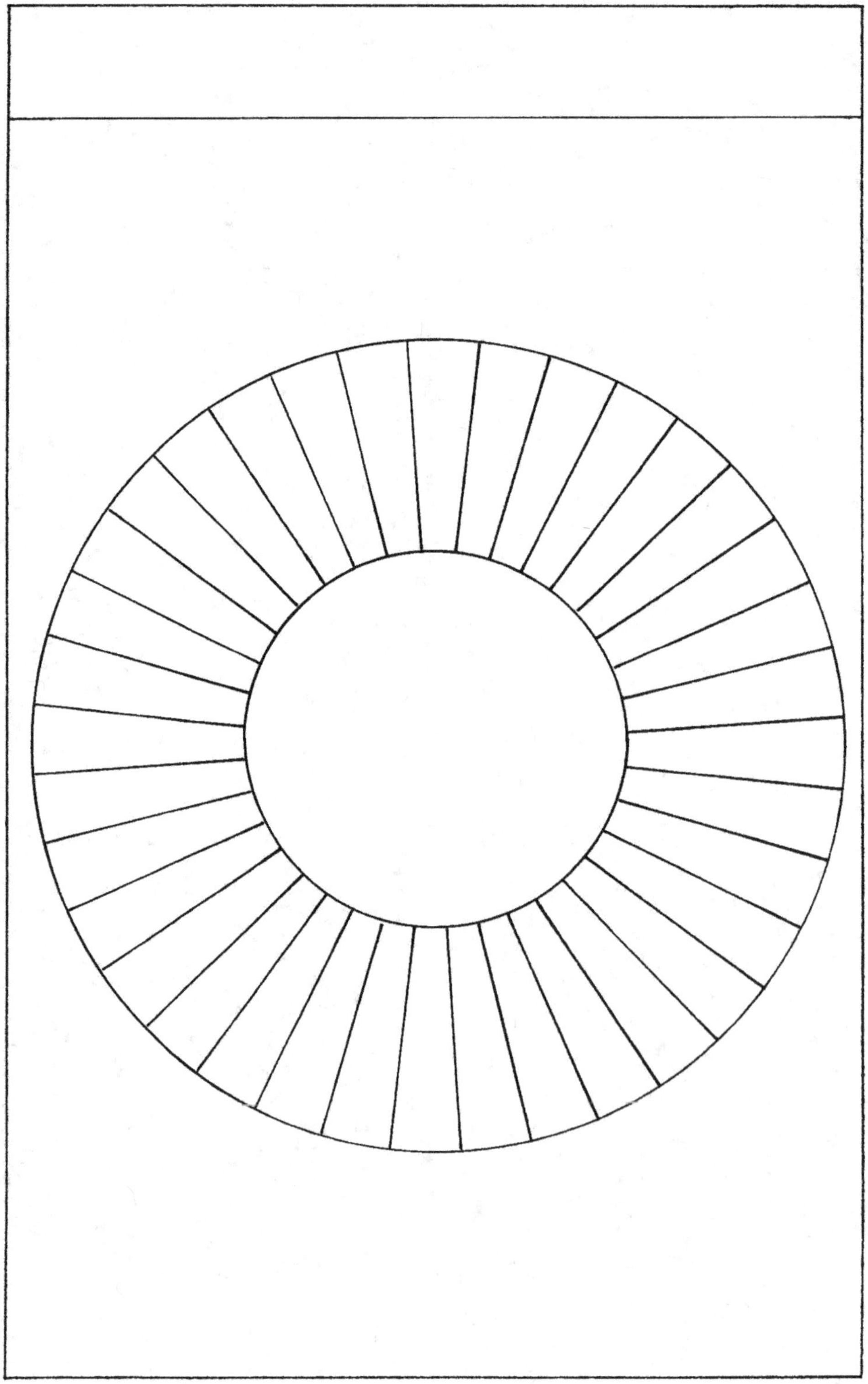

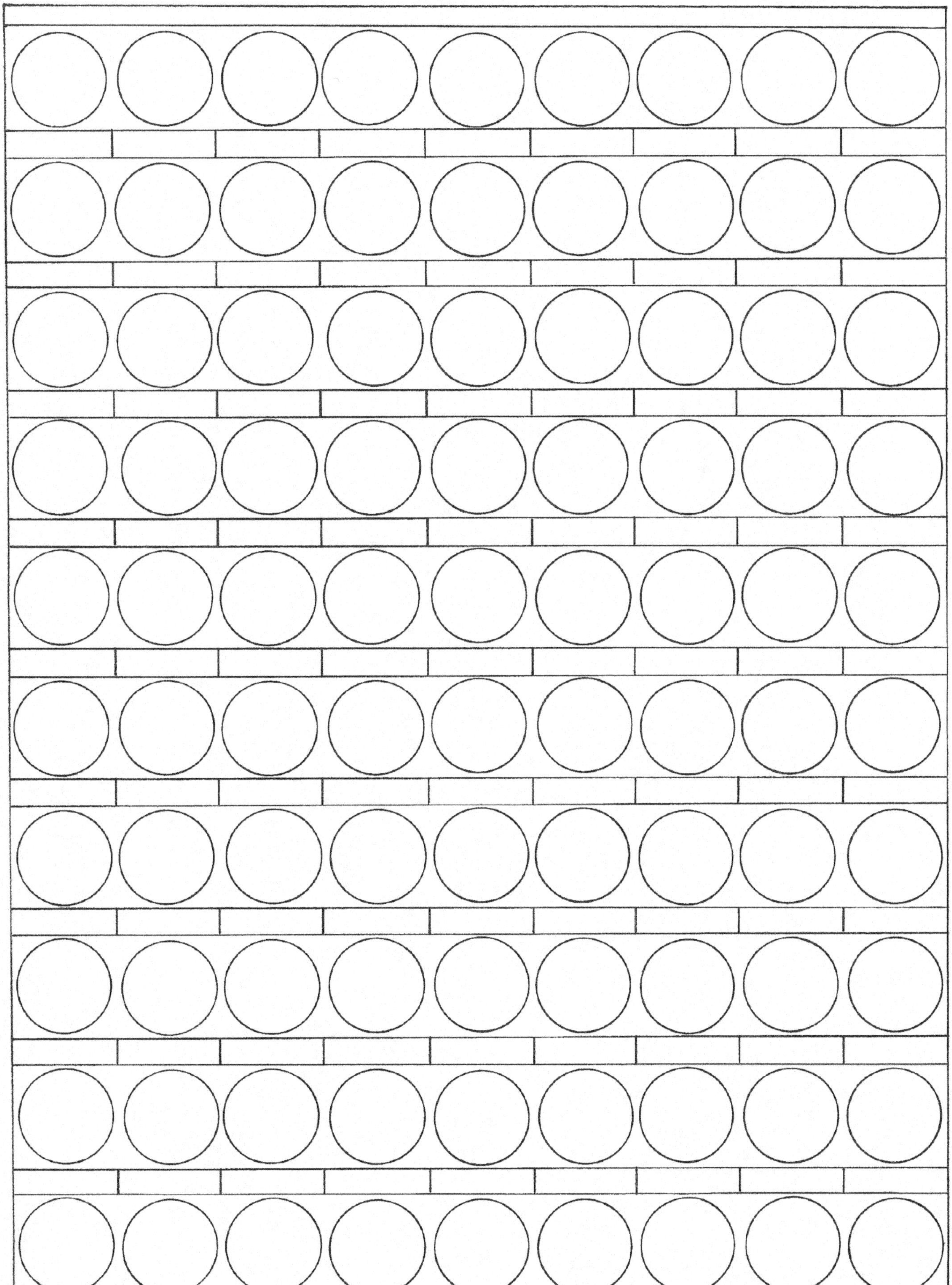

www.ingramcontent.com/pod-product-compliance
Lightning Source LLC
Chambersburg PA
CBHW081118240526
45470CB00019B/2612
* 9 7 8 8 7 7 2 0 1 0 9 7 7 *